ORVIS®

The Orvis Guide to
BETTER
FLY CASTING
A Problem-Solving Approach

AL KYTE

THE LYONS PRESS
Guilford, Connecticut
An imprint of The Globe Pequot Press

The Lyons Press is an imprint of The Globe Pequot Press.

Illustrations by Julie Ecklund

Photographs by Rex Agbulos

Designed by Maggie Peterson

Library of Congress Cataloging-in-Publication data is available on file.

ISBN 978-1-59228-870-0

Printed in China

10 9 8 7 6 5 4 3 2 1

CONTENTS

Why write a book about fly casting? There are plenty of books on "how to cast." A new casting book should offer something more, but what?

Fly-fishing guide Art Teter recently suggested that casting books should get back to the business of helping fishermen. Casting instructor Michael Maloney went further in saying that we need a book that teaches people to *solve their own* on-the-water casting problems.

Authors have been doing this to some degree, by offering various specialty casts or trouble shooting tips. But these approaches apparently fall short because of the many specialty casts or corrections you read about, it is too easy to forget which ones apply to the problem you suddenly find yourself experiencing. It would be more helpful to have just one problem-solving approach for whatever casting problem comes up as you fish.

What would that problem-solving approach look like? It would need to start with an understanding of the problem you face—how to present your line, leader, and fly properly in that situation. Of the three, the fly line is the most important because the leader and fly follow its path. Since your fly line goes where the rod tip directs it, you therefore also need to know how to vary your fly rod's movements to achieve that presentation. I believe this is the key to correcting any problems, because the fly rod is the adjustable link between your hand's movements and your fly line's movements. This brings us to the object of our focus: a systematic way of changing and controlling the various ways a fly rod moves. Giving you the means to apply this to your fishing is the intent of this book.

You have probably figured out that this is not primarily a book for beginning fly fishers. If it were, I would lovingly expand on the basic content presented in Part I and go no further. The people who stand to gain the most from this book already know what a casting loop is and have caught enough fish on a fly to regard themselves as fly fishers. If you are such an angler, you already have the experience to benefit both from the new information presented here and the unusual openness to differences in casting styles. This book should also be helpful if you have been looking for a way to teach the sport you love to someone else. On the other hand, I probably should not discourage beginners too much, because I have known some who could apply many of these ideas and techniques to their own learning.

How can I prepare you to solve your own casting problems? Certainly you need some knowledge to help guide the casting adjustments you will need to make. The most useful knowledge has to do with how you vary the fly rod's movements to change the tip's path. I offer this primarily through four rod movements I call "variables": speed, stroke length, angular rotation, and up/down tilt. If I can help you to adjust and control these rod variables as well as a few others, I will have given you important tools you can use to find solutions to any on-the-water casting problems you may encounter. Eventually, you should need only to adjust the rod in certain practiced ways—and then watch how the line, leader, and fly respond.

The development of this approach starts in Part I with my presentation of a short overhead cast (i.e., twelve feet of fly line and a leader beyond the rod's tip). This is more than just a review; I want you to examine your own short cast to eliminate as much wasted motion as possible. You might just learn to do more with less. If you do not have an efficient casting stroke to start with, it may be difficult to make the adjustments it will take to progress. As you rework your short cast, you will also become familiar with these four primary rod variables.

In Part II, your purpose shifts from short line control to casting for distance. The changes you make when doing this should begin to give you a sense of the importance of these four rod movements and why I refer to them as *variables*. As you work on ways to improve your long casts, you also become familiar with how to change each of these movements to keep your rod tip and fly line moving along a straight path.

The emphasis in Part III shifts to practicing these four rod movements as well as a few others I add. With each of these movements, you practice by going from one extreme to the other—sometimes from one type of error to another. For example, if you are working on how much speed to apply to the rod, you gradually move from applying too little speed, through the correct range, to applying too much speed, and then work back to the

opposite extreme. In this type of practice, you see for yourself how your fly line, leader, and fly move differently as that rod movement changes. So, as you learn to control these various rod movements—one at a time—you are also learning how to gain control over the movements of your line and leader.

Then you start combining these rod variables in your practice and learn which ones work together to move your fly line in predictable ways. You are adding to the adjustments you need to solve casting problems in your fishing.

Finally, you are ready to start using these rod adjustments to test your problem-solving ability. You are given a number of common casting problems you might experience when fishing. After reading each problem, you are invited to pick up your fly rod, go out to your casting area, and set up as realistic a situation as you can to test that problem. If you feel you need to review these movements, you don't need to reread anything: just use the warm-up practice you are given, going through the exaggerated movements associated with each rod variable. Then experiment with the most promising rod movements to find the combination that best solves that casting problem.

Put your fly rod aside, return to this book, and look up my solution to that problem. How different is your solution from mine? You may decide you like your answer better. Sometimes there is more than one way to solve a problem, including using several rod movements in combination. The more you practice *casting to situations,* the more you might find yourself thinking about problems and solutions that are more complicated than those I have presented. Perhaps, one day, you will write the book that takes this process to a new level.

Part I

BETTER BASIC CAST

CHAPTER 1

WHAT IS A BETTER CAST?

Wherever my travels take me, I see people who could use help with their casting. Many of them catch fish and may even think of themselves as skillful fly fishers. However, they often lack the casting skills to reach some of their fish or make the adjustments to present the fly differently. There is a lot to know about fly casting that could help such anglers. Fly fishing may be the only form of rod and reel angling that has books devoted entirely to the casting part. Anglers who cast a fly well have usually read articles or books on casting, received personal help, and spent hours practicing. Yet many people today seem unwilling to pay for a series of fly casting lessons. They will pay for equipment and for the fly fishing experience, but not for the skill it takes to use the equipment effectively during that fishing. Instead, they expect their fishing guides to be miracle workers. It seems as if there is an unwritten law that states, "You don't pay money to practice fishing." Realizing this, I have decided to try a different approach, one that helps anglers solve their own casting problems. If you skipped the preface to this book, I suggest you read it now to get an understanding of how I intend to do this.

WHAT DOES A BETTER CAST LOOK LIKE?

This book is about better fly casting—and getting better starts with being able to recognize a good cast when you see one. What does a really good fly cast look like? What are its characteristics? Let's start with an overhead cast.

It is the cast you use most often in your fishing, as well as the foundation movement for most specialty casts. Artists have sought to capture its beauty—the essential grace of a fly cast—in the smooth unrolling of a fly line overhead.

Although the overhead cast is basic, its movements can be difficult to master, particularly as you add distance. The best picture of a good cast may come from watching experts such as Lefty Kreh, Mel Krieger, Steve Rajeff, or Joan Wulff. The problem is that such experts often have different casting motions and teaching language, some of which seem contradictory. This can be confusing not only to fly casting students but to instructors as well. It can leave you wondering who or what really defines good casting form.

Differences in the cast. If you watch casters closely, you will see differences in how they stand, grip the rod, and move their casting arm and body. When such different movements result in good casts, you begin to realize that they might not be incorrect. Such individual differences are what I call *acceptable variations.*

You may also see the fly rod doing different things—being moved through wide or narrow angles, tilted to cast higher or lower, moved quickly or slowly, bent very little or almost double, or the rod's butt moved a few inches or a few feet. Under the right circumstances any of these differences can produce good casts.

So, understanding a better cast requires broadening your point of view to make room for different styles and physical characteristics of casters, different casting purposes, and even different equipment. For example, a tall, heavy person will have different casting advantages and movements than a short, quick-moving person. As your casting purpose shifts from line control of a short cast to throwing for distance, you are likely to shift from shorter to longer movements, slower to faster movements, fewer to more body parts, and from a lower to higher point of

aim. And a 10-weight fly rod will require more force and perhaps even different muscles than your 4- or 5-weight trout rod. So, you discover that good form in casting is not limited to a certain *look,* but it will vary from one caster to the next—even in the same person casting different amounts of line.

Beyond the differences. If the movements of both the casters and fly rods can be so different, what remains the same to help define and give structure to an overhead cast? In the studies I did with biomechanics professor Gary Moran, what stayed the same was *straightening and unrolling the fly line back and forth along a straight path overhead.* That included several parts—positioning the back cast directly back from the forward cast, accelerating the rod tip along a straight path, and stopping the rod tip close below that path for a tight unrolling "loop" of the fly line (figure 1-1). So, in this better cast you can vary your own movements and those of the fly rod as long as they contribute to moving the fly line along a straight path. So you have a range of correctness as well as a common focus.

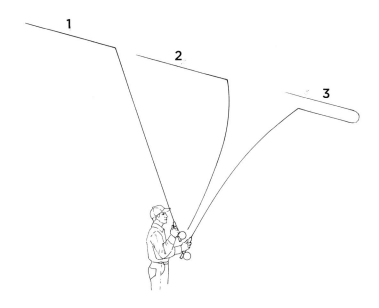

Figure 1-1. Straight line flow.

The fly rod. You already know that a fly rod—through its length, lightness, and flexibility—can effectively deliver a fly line over distance. But your fly rod has another less understood role as well: adjusting to make corrections. To move the fly line along a straight path, your rod's tip, which directs the movement of that line, also needs to be controlled along that same path (figure 1-2). To do that with different fly rods and over different casting distances, you must bend that rod just the right amount and precisely adjust its angular change, forward movement, speed, and timing. You continually adjust this flexible rod in these ways to control what your fly line does.

So, when solving casting problems in your fishing, you watch the fly line, leader, and fly to see how well you are accomplishing what you set out to do. Based on what you see, you may need to vary what the fly rod does. You *observe* and *adjust*. And most fly fishers are not prepared to do that in any systematic way. So increasing your awareness first, then your ability to control what your fly rod does provides an important key to achieving your better cast—one that puts the fly line, leader, and fly exactly where you want. What you learn in the pages of this book should help you progress toward becoming a master of your fly rod.

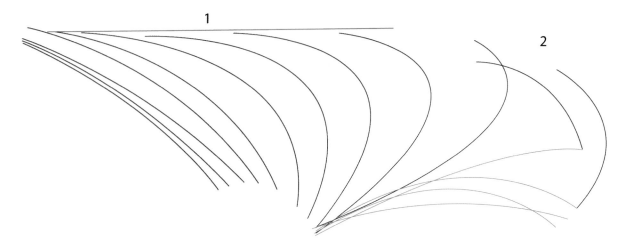

Figure 1-2. Sequential rod movements during a forward cast show (1) the rod tip following a straight path as the bend increases before (2) dropping down to form a loop in the fly line during the release of that bend.

CHAPTER 2

ELEMENTS OF STYLE IN THE OVERHEAD CAST

"Let the rod do the work!" This familiar casting advice suggests that it is the rod that does the work in casting. What is more accurate to say is that in order to get more out of your fly rod, you, the caster, must learn to work more efficiently. Before discussing ways of adjusting your rod to do that, it might help you to know some of the choices you have in your own casting movements.

Casting instructors teach different grips, stances, and casting movements; yet too often, they give the impression that their way is the only "correct" one. It has worked for them, so it must be best for everyone. Yet, I have used various stances, grips, and arm movements to cast and believe you learn more from thinking of these differences in terms of their *advantages* and *disadvantages* rather than as being right or wrong. You will probably find your best grip, stance, and casting movements after considering the advantages of various styles in relation to your own body build, movements, and type of fly fishing—and then by doing some experimenting. Some differences in casting style can be traced back to how you start a cast: how you stand and hold the rod.

CASTING GRIPS

Skilled fly fishers sometimes grip the rod in a certain way based upon their hand size, and sometimes because they look for different performance characteristics from their casts. Someone who fishes small streams with short casts wants delicacy and looks for a grip that

brings sensitivity—increased feel of the rod tip. Someone who fishes more in salt water might look for a grip that provides the strength to force bend into a stiff rod to straighten as much line as possible.

Some years ago, I taught fly casting to an orthopedic surgeon who specialized in the hand and arm. He sent me several medical articles that indicated that three fingers—the middle, ring, and little fingers—together make up our *grasping fingers*. How you add the index finger and thumb to this grasp depends on the purpose of your movement. If you want strength, the index finger and thumb are usually positioned close to the other fingers, often in a fist-like grip, giving support behind the primary direction of movement. However, if you want to emphasize sensitivity or *feel*, you are more likely to extend the index finger and thumb to some extent. In both cases, the rod handle runs diagonally across the palm of your hand. I consider this trade-off between sensitivity and strength to be important in evaluating casting grips.

Grips are typically pictured, described, and taught with the reel on the underside of a fly rod that is pointed forward—as if you have not yet made your first back cast. Thus a thumb-on-top grip would seem to always be raised upward during the back cast to provide thumb support behind the forward cast. However, some casters turn or rotate the hand outward during the back cast and may make the forward cast with the reel positioned out to the side. This further complicates the notion of grip, because the hand position during the cast is then different from the one taught to start the movement. The casting grip I analyze is the one that does the work—the hand position that moves the cast forward.

Thumb-on-top grip. I believe that most casting instructors in this country teach the thumb-on-top grip with the index finger slightly separated from the others, in the position of a "trigger" finger. Lefty Kreh uses the thumb as a directional guide in much of his instruction. I start

Thumb-on-top grip.

beginning students with this grip because it offers a balance between strength and sensitivity. I like its versatility.

Extended-finger grip. As I observe my students casting, I may have a few of them experiment with other grips. If a muscular student applies more force than necessary, I might suggest an extended-finger grip for a more sensitive feel of the rod. Although extending the forefinger has been thought of as a weak grip, Bob Jacklin, Gary Borger, and some European experts use versions of it to throw impressively long casts with trout-weight rods.

Knuckle-on-top grip. There is some disagreement as to which is the strongest grip. Putting the thumb on top brings strong muscles into play; however, rotating the knuckle of the index finger toward the top provides rigid support from the bones of the hand. Tim Rajeff and Ed Mosser are among the distance tournament casters who have preferred this grip. One advantage is that this grip

Extended-finger grip.

allows you to move your casting hand well back for a long cast without having to rotate the reel out to the side. It is the only grip that provides adequate support behind the rod when my fingers and thumb have become cold enough to lose strength. (Sometimes I don't have the sense to stop fishing when I should.)

In my fishing, I sometimes switch from a thumb grip to an extended-finger to emphasize sensitive tip control on short casts, or rotate the knuckle of the index finger to the top when making long casts. Some fly fishers cast with variations of these distinctive grips. Yet with any grip, it is possible to hold the rod too tightly. One old saying recommends holding the rod as if holding a bird in the hand—tightly enough to keep it from escaping, but not so tight as to squeeze it.

CASTING STANCES

Squared stance. The stance you use for casting can influence the movements that follow, such as how you move

Knuckle-on-top grip.

your casting arm and add force with your shoulder and body. I like to start beginning students with a *squared stance,* because I believe it is best suited to teaching the arm movement I prefer. In a squared stance you face the target squarely without dropping either foot back. Keeping your arm in alignment with your target direction throughout the back cast and forward cast helps keep the fly line from veering off to the left or right. Straight-line movement of the rod hand, elbow, rod tip, and fly line is a concern whether viewing your cast from the side or front.

Open stance. Some casting instructors start their students with the casting side dropped back, as if the student was preparing to throw a ball. This is sometimes called an *open stance.* The ease of learning timing is an advantage of this stance. When you are able to watch your back cast, you can see when to start forward. Yet, this stance invites the shoulders and hips to rotate, which can easily rotate a beginning caster's arm, fly rod, and

Squared stance.

fly line out of alignment as well. Having to realign your arm and rod for the forward cast complicates your movement, particularly if you are trying to keep your casting elbow forward.

I believe most students learn timing best by turning back to see the fly line straightening behind them. For this reason, I invite students with timing problems to turn and look back—opening up the stance just enough to see the back cast. I return them to a squared stance as soon as the timing problem has been corrected. You may turn to watch a back cast at times when practicing, but seldom do so when fishing. This is the origin of the adage, "Watching your back cast is bad form, except in grizzly bear country." I have to laugh because one morning in Alaska I happened to turn back to watch a back cast and did notice a big bear moving toward me along the shoreline. Fortunately the salmon were abundant.

As students progress to longer casts, I encourage them to drop their casting side back to take advantage of

Open stance, casting side back.

the longer hand movements that this stance invites. By this time, casting habits have been well formed, and arm alignment no longer concerns me as much. This stance allows you to watch your loops forming off the rod tip on a back cast, which is a great way to learn how and where to stop the rod butt to form small loops in a long back-cast line. Bruce Richards, a highly regarded instructor from the Midwest, first introduced me to this technique.

Closed stance. Occasionally I see a person with the casting side and foot forward, rather than back. I see this *closed stance* most often in top tournament casters, when working on accuracy. Turning the casting side forward brings the hand and arm that direct the cast into closer alignment with a line between the caster's eyes and the target. When attempting an accurate cast, I sometimes find myself using this stance to line up my eyes, hand, and point of aim. It begins to resemble the form we see in most skilled dart throwers.

Closed stance, casting side forward.

Although I start students with the grip and stance I believe work best for most people—a squared stance, with the thumb providing support behind the forward cast—this is a *style* choice, and not the only correct technique. I let some of my students switch to other styles at times. The art of teaching has more to do with helping each student find a way of moving that is both successful and enjoyable rather than insisting on one way of doing something.

THE BACK CAST

"God must not be a fly fisher, or He would have put eyes in the back of our heads." My student was clearly frustrated with her back cast. "I'm not so sure," I smiled. "Maybe He just wants us to have faith in what we cannot see." She grumbled something and returned to her casting.

Many people share this frustration with a form of angling in which the line is cast backward before being cast forward. Even accomplished fly fishers are sometimes self-conscious about their back casts. You don't want to keep looking back when you are fishing, and few people are used to applying force backward when throwing something. Most people underpower the back cast at first, while others jerk the rod back with too much force. The most common error, though, is dropping the rod tip and fly line low in back by breaking the wrist. This is so common among beginning *and experienced* fly fishers that much of my teaching is directed toward preventing it.

Preparatory movement. You start the back cast with the rod tip pointed forward and low to the water or grass on which the fly line lays. Any slack in the line has been stripped in. This gives that fly line the straightest possible path down through the rod and onto the water. The lack of slack allows you to start the line moving and the rod bending with your first lifting movement. Starting with the rod tip low also provides the most room above the rod in which to lift it, to direct the line into an upward angle behind you. Any slack in that line would delay the start of the line's movement until later in the back cast, which would result in stopping farther back as well—probably dropping the line low behind you.

Lift the rod slowly until the rod tip is high enough— perhaps halfway up to vertical—to be able to move fast along a straight back-cast path. Although I consider this steady lift to be preparatory to the cast in one sense, it does start the rod bending and the line moving smoothly. Starting too quickly from this low starting position could shock the rod and bend it so much that the tip drops below the path of the fly line, causing a *tailing loop* (figure 2-1). Early speed also causes the "whooshing" sound you may hear your rod make, as well as a trail of bubbles you see on the water if you have lifted the line off too early. When your rod tip is about halfway to vertical, you make your back cast in a fast, smooth movement to a stop.

Arm movement styles. The two general styles I have seen experts use for moving the casting arm back are overhead and sidearm. In both styles you try to send the fly line back and upward enough to straighten behind your next forward cast. Lefty Kreh is among those who have taught more of a sidearm back cast, moving the hand and rod back along a nearly horizontal plane—upward just enough to direct the fly line back at an upward angle. I see this sidearm style of back cast used mainly in salt water where you sometimes need to keep big hooks away from your head in the wind and may want to avoid lifting heavy, stiff rods overhead.

In the more common back-cast style, you lift the rod back overhead. I prefer to start my teaching with this movement, because you are able to keep the back cast and forward cast in the same plane, which simplifies directional control for a beginner.

If you use an overhead back cast, you should move your hand and rod upward, rather than horizontally, to take advantage of how a fly rod unloads. If you move your hand back *horizontally* to stop an overhead cast, the rod's tip bends backward and downward, which directs the fly line back low and with big loops. However, when you stop an *upward-moving* rod abruptly, much of the tip's bend gets absorbed down into the middle of the rod when the bend is reversed. The tip still has some backward bend, but much less downward bend. This explained to me why Tim Rajeff can rotate his wrist as much as he does, yet still cast such small back-cast loops.

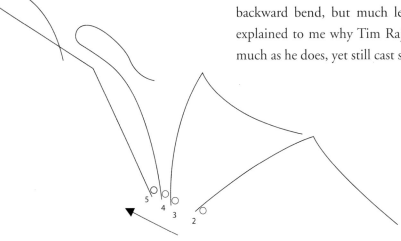

Figure 2-1. Back-cast sequence with (1-2) initial rod lift, (2-3) line "dip" from excessive rod bend, (3-4) outward progression of that dip, and (4-5) resulting "tail."

His wrist action is accompanied by an arm lift that allows the rod to unload while moving upward.

The direction and distance your rod hand moves to make a back cast usually varies with the amount of fly line you need to straighten in back. On a short cast, your movement is short—typically up to chin level—and more upward than back. On longer casts, your movement is longer—up to ear level or higher—and more backward than upward. This additional movement lifts your hand far enough to set up a stronger throwing position for a longer forward cast. To set up this arm position, I often teach students to lift "clear to the ear" or "answer the phone" on the back cast. Lifting your hand to ear level raises your elbow a few inches, which positions the arm to use large shoulder muscles for a strong forward cast.

Wrist styles. I also see differences in the way a caster's wrist is used during the back cast. Some experts use a little *controlled* wrist motion to increase the speed of the back cast. Joan Wulff has her wrist crack slightly near the end of the back cast, while Tim Rajeff uses wrist motion earlier in his lift. Both throw beautiful back casts.

However, adding wrist motion to the back cast also can detract from the control you have over that movement. I have seen enough students lose consistency when taught even a limited wrist movement on the back cast, so I start beginners with a very firm wrist. I like Steve Rajeff's back cast as a model for beginners. It is difficult to detect any wrist movement in his lift until he has stopped the rod's butt. So I leave the introduction of additional wrist motion and tip speed for later.

What I dread seeing most in experienced anglers I am asked to teach is a low, wristy back-cast motion. Most of us do not have enough strength in the muscles that control our wrist to apply force smoothly to a long cast, and this movement habit is seldom easy to break.

An abrupt stop. As your hand approaches your stop position, make that stop abruptly. Whenever you do, you force the tip to speed up and reverse its bend. This speeds up the fly line as well. After the stop, your wrist may open slightly in preparation for the forward cast.

So the back-cast movement I teach to *beginning* students is a smooth, firm-wristed lift. This movement emphasizes control in the movement of a fly line that is back out of your view. When I think of a firm wrist

Stopping an overhead back cast with an upward hand and rod movement invites the reverse bend to be absorbed down into the rod's butt (1) rather than in a downward-bending tip (2), which increases loop size.

I sometimes smile when recalling the advice that Mel Krieger so often gives students at the end of the first day of a two-day fly fishing school: "Sleep with a firm wrist."

THE FORWARD CAST

The overhead cast is two casts in one, a back cast and a forward cast. The back cast, though demanding of your attention and practice time, is essentially a movement that comes before—a way to straighten the line behind your cast toward the fish.

One of the most satisfying things about casting forward is watching your best loops move out from the rod tip. Of course those loops look different when watching someone else's cast from the side than when watching your own cast. So it helps students if you give them feedback on what their various casting loops look like as they occur. They can also gain this self-teaching visual perspective by standing as close behind you as possible while you cast various types of loops.

Start smoothly. You start your forward cast when your back-cast line has *almost* straightened behind you. If you hear a whip-cracking sound as you cast forward, you started forward too early—while the line was still moving rapidly backward. If you feel a tug after your back cast, you have waited too long; your line has straightened and is starting to drop. If you wait this long when using a heavily weighted fly, it will swing up and down when being pulled forward and may hit and even hook you.

Your fly line will not always straighten behind you, especially if there is wind. So your initial forward movement may have to help pull the line straight, as well as start it moving. Any unevenness in this initial pull on the line, as from punching or shocking the rod, will cause the line to move away from its straight path. So instructors use words such as *gradually* and *smoothly* to describe the initial movement forward.

Some anglers, when losing the feel of the back-cast fly line, start moving or *creeping* the rod tip forward

A "tailing tendency" in the line flow on top reveals uneven force application. The bottom photo shows a good parallel casting loop.

before applying force to make the forward cast. This attempt to regain the feel of the line wastes some of the movement needed to make the forward cast. With too little of the rod's movement still available for the cast itself, people tend to jerk the rod forward rather than move smoothly. Check to make sure you are holding your rod absolutely still between your back cast and the start of your forward cast.

People move their casting arm differently during the forward cast. Yet every impressive distance caster I have analyzed, regardless of style, uses some type of shoulder movement to provide a smooth start to the forward line flow. When casters lose their smoothness during longer casts, it is usually from using the wrist to start forward. This may be the most common cause of tailing loops among experienced fly fishers. Weak wrist muscles are better suited for quick, final movements than for those requiring sustained, evenly applied force. A tailing loop occurs in an overhead cast when the rod tip or any of the line coming behind it dips below the path of the moving fly line. When I certify a casting instructor's performance, I do not even want to see a tailing tendency in the basic overhead cast.

One style of arm movement. The shoulder movement I prefer to start students with lifts the elbow on the back cast, then lowers it four to six inches on the forward cast. The elbow remains bent and the wrist firm in this compact movement (figure 2-2). Dropping your elbow to start the forward movement also starts rotating your rod butt and moving the fly line without any jerking or unevenness. Gary and Jason Borger teach this shoulder movement by having their students think of using gravity to lower the arm a little at the start of the forward cast. While not the most natural movement for some people to learn, it provides smooth line flow for those who can pick it up. Later in this book, I go further into a description of several styles of arm movement commonly used to make a long forward cast.

Figure 2-2. Shoulder movement starts the rod tip (and line) forward smoothly.

Styles of stopping the rod. In addition to teaching people to start the cast smoothly, most instructors also emphasize stopping the cast abruptly. Yet, even then, teachers differ in how much wrist to use and in how to teach that final wrist movement.

Most instructors teach a *firm* wrist throughout the forward cast to reduce the expected "wristiness," but they probably hope students will move the wrist enough to help speed up the tip. I am careful to avoid the term *locked wrist,* because some students do exactly what you say and then have trouble loosening their grip enough to use the wrist at all. And if you even mention wrist movement in your teaching, students will often overdo it. Knowing this, some instructors teach students to *press the thumb.* In doing so, they teach a little late wrist motion without having students even think about the wrist.

Other instructors believe the wrist is important enough to emphasize in their teaching. Longtime Orvis

1

2

3

Produce fast-moving casting loops by starting the forward cast (1) by dropping the elbow (2) before "breaking" the wrist (3).

master instructor Bill Cairns has taught tightening the thumb and forefinger, bringing the wrist into play and stopping. Doug Swisher referred to this quick wrist movement as a *micro-wrist,* and Joe Humphries refers to it as a *tap.* I have sometimes taught a more deliberate "drop the elbow, break the wrist" sequence—which enables chronic wristy casters to channel their wrist movement into a later time frame within the cast.

Jimmy Green also emphasized pressing with the thumb to create a little wrist movement before stopping it almost immediately against the heel of his hand. So the "positive" in his positive stop is a little wrist pivot *that not only stops the rod, but helps force the tip over the resistance of the butt of the rod.* When I want to tighten up my own casting loops, I bring this teaching to mind.

So I emphasize wrist firmness when introducing the back cast, but intentionally build in a wrist pivot to stop the forward cast.

THE FOLLOW DOWN

This abrupt stop ends your forward cast. The rod tip should straighten again close beneath the moving fly line. If, instead, you drop the rod tip low during the cast, you pull the lower part of the casting loop open and may lose your small loop. Yet after you stop the cast, you can lower your hand and rod for fishing or starting the next back cast. Some instructors call this the *follow down.* Another term used to set apart the initial high stop from the delayed lowering of the rod is *stop and drop.* This follow down is not generally considered to be part of the cast.

CHAPTER 3

THE SHORT OVERHEAD CAST

A lifetime of teaching physical education and coaching athletes has pounded into me the importance of starting simply—whether teaching an overhead cast, baseball throw, basketball shot, or tennis forehand. Start short until you have control over what is happening to your arm, body, and whatever you are holding. When you believe you can handle something more, add movements that contribute to greater speed or distance. This has worked best for most of the people I have taught and coached.

The short overhead cast is what many of us started with on the creeks of our youth, and it becomes the building block for the longer overhead casts you need on bigger waters. It is the cast I use to start teaching how to vary what you do with your fly rod.

Years ago, when I first taught intermediate and advanced fly fishing classes, I could not wait to get past my review of the basic overhead cast to excite people with the fun of distance and specialty casts. Yet the longer I taught, the more time I spent with these experienced fly fishers on their basic cast. The advanced casts just had to wait. I had begun to realize that there was no sense in moving into advanced techniques as long as the foundation was shaky. The problems observed in a person's short cast would not go away by themselves, and they often became magnified with the additional demands of more complicated casts. So for me, the journey to a better cast starts by making your short cast as solid as possible.

How short is short? I believe that most casting instructors start with a cast that lands the fly twenty-five to thirty feet from where you are standing, with the idea of providing enough line weight beyond the rod's tip to allow you to feel that rod loading (i.e., bending against the resistance of the fly line). That was my thinking as well—until I helped Jimmy Green teach an elementary class at a Federation of Fly Fishers (FFF) international conclave some years back. I had been looking forward to spending time with this man who had been so well thought of as a tournament caster, rod designer, and casting instructor.

In fact, a few years earlier, fifteen of us "casting experts" from around the country had been brought together to start the FFF's casting instructor certification program. I remember wondering how experts such as Joan Wulff, Lefty Kreh, Mel Krieger, Steve Rajeff, Doug Swisher, Leon Chandler, Jim Green, and a few others would interact on the same committee. What ended up impressing me most was the obvious respect these experts all had for Jim Green. When he spoke, they became quiet and listened.

So I was interested to learn how Jim taught an elementary casting class. The biggest difference from my own teaching was evident almost immediately. Here was a man who could cast a long line as effortlessly and beautifully as anyone, yet he started his students with only 12 feet of fly line and a 7½-foot leader beyond the rod tip. As I thought about that, I began to see some advantages. The short line permitted him to start students comfortably with a short, simple casting motion and, perhaps even more important, with the best control I had seen of an upward-angled back cast. You don't have to teach fly casting very long to realize how important it is to do whatever you can to prevent beginners from dropping their back casts low. The short line helped.

But how do you load a rod with so little line? Jim's students had no trouble doing so, because his teaching emphasized movements that limited the rod's bending to the tip section. This provided all the flexing power necessary to load and unroll a few feet of fly line. In fact, any additional movement is wasted motion that detracts from the sensitive feel and pleasure of a short cast. Although I didn't realize it at the time, I was getting an important lesson in short-line casting efficiency, of using as few parts as it takes to do the job.

Efficiency of a short overhead cast. The short hand movement limited both the distance and angle of the rod butt's movement. Limiting this movement and abruptly stopping the rod forced the energy of the cast up into the more flexible tip. This is an important, often overlooked fact: to emphasize the tip's movement, you reduce the movement in the rod's butt. Most beginners and too many experienced fly fishers move the rod's butt too far in a short cast. It helps some people to think of the fly rod as being made up of two levers: a butt lever and a tip lever. To emphasize the movement in the tip lever, you stop the movement in the butt lever.

For years, Mel Krieger has emphasized *tip casting* in his teaching. His approach progressed from teaching students to cast off the tip of the rod, to casting off its middle, and finally to casting off the butt of the rod. He started students tip casting with a very short cast and kept adding line until there was not enough strength in the rod's tip to unroll and straighten the weight of the line. He had them widen the angle of the cast enough to bend the rod down into its middle. This allowed them to keep adding line until that much movement failed to straighten the forward cast. Then he had the students widen the angle even more to invite bend down into the butt of the rod, providing additional strength to straighten even a longer line. Only when I began to teach in guide schools did I realize how few fly fishers have been taught to cast off different parts of the rod. I found, for example, that some boat guides spend their season attempting to teach various clients one cast—a cast of thirty to forty feet angled forward ahead of a drifting boat. When all the casts are so similar, you may not even think in terms of the rod adjustments to control different lengths of line. I don't blame the guides, because they are forced to select something quick to teach that will help people catch a few fish. Too many people who hire guides have not learned enough about using their fly rods beforehand.

For several years I headed up the casting part of the guide school at the annual Orvis Rendezvous in the Rocky Mountains. I was fortunate to work under Mark Bressler, and to have two co-teachers—Hutch Hutchinson and Lori Ann Murphy—who were not only excellent casters and enthusiastic teachers but also people open to teaching approaches I brought over from other sports. The three of us were able to excite the fishing guides with a casting program very different from what they were accustomed to. One thing I recall is that many of those guides dramatically improved their short casts by cutting back on their hand, arm, and rod butt movements—and in so doing, they began to feel the rod tip working for the first time.

ROD VARIABLES

The casting changes just discussed are three of the most important adjustments you make in moving a fly rod. I refer to these characteristics as *rod bend, angular rotation,* and *stroke length.* Old-timers would sometimes refer to rod bend as the *spring* of the cast and angular rotation and stroke length together as the *swing* of the cast. The swing is the part of the movement that would still be present if you were casting a rigid broomstick.

Rod bend. When people speak of loading and unloading the fly rod, they are referring to the bend that occurs in the rod when you move it against the resistance of a straightened fly line, called loading (figure 3-1), and the

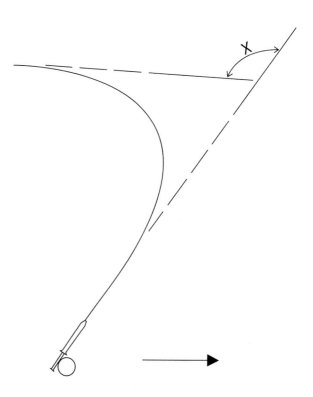

Figure 3-1. Measuring rod bend.

release of that bend in stopping the rod, called unloading. In this book, I have you increase or decrease the amount of bend you put into the rod by varying the amount of hand speed you use during your cast. In the previous discussion on tip casting a short line, little speed was used and the bend was limited to the tip section by stopping the rod after a very short movement.

Angular rotation. When a cast is viewed from the side, you see the fly rod's butt changing angles in the way a spoke of a wheel changes angles when rotated about an axle. I refer to this angular change as *angular rotation.* This angular dimension of the rod's movement has sometimes been called the casting *arc.* I avoid using the word arc because it also means a curving line, which has confused too many people. Authors and teachers have also used a clock face to help visualize rod angle changes, particularly where the rod starts and stops the cast. I also avoid using clock positions as much as possible because

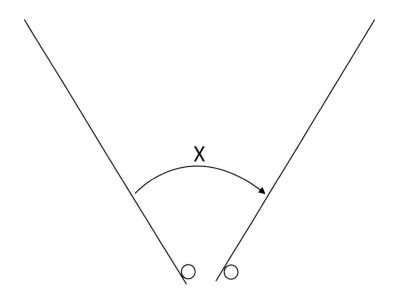

Figure 3-2. Measuring angular rotation.

people start believing that certain positions, such as ten to two o'clock, apply to all their casting and fishing. That is the opposite of what I am trying to get across. It is important to think of angular rotation as something you vary from one cast to the next for different casting and fishing conditions. We measure this rod angle at the part of the rod that stays the straightest during the cast—the butt section (figure 3-2). My primary concern here is to teach you to be able to increase or decrease the angle of movement covered by the rod during a cast. In the previous discussion on short-line efficiency, the angular rotation of the butt was minimized to help transfer the energy of the cast up into the rod's tip section.

Stroke length. In addition to bending the rod and rotating its angle of movement, you also move the entire rod some distance toward the casting direction. The distance the fly rod moves forward during the cast is best measured from the butt end of the fly rod—the only part that can

be kept separate from the changes that are occurring in the rod angle or bend (figure 3-3). For practical purposes, this is the same distance as your forward hand stroke. So,

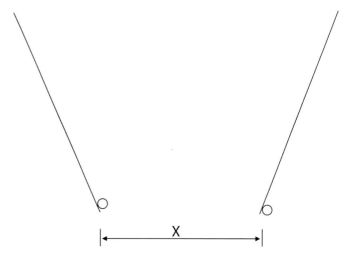

Figure 3-3. Measuring stroke length.

in the research Gary Moran and I published in 1993, we coined the term *stroke length* for this forward movement of the rod butt or casting hand. Prior to our study, stroke length had been used vaguely in the casting literature without communicating any clear or consistent idea of what was meant. There was nothing measurable. In this book, think of changing stroke length by either shortening or lengthening the distance your hand moves the rod in the direction of the cast. In the short-cast discussion earlier in the chapter, stroke length was kept short to help emphasize movement in the rod's tip.

Up/down tilt—raising or lowering the target line. This rod variable has to do with the direction you intend to straighten the fly line. Although you could think of changing a target direction by aiming more to the left or right, here you are changing the upward or downward direction your line moves forward from your rod tip. To raise or lower that direction, you tilt your casting stroke

forward or back. This means changing the position or angle in which you stop the rod on both back cast and forward cast. Try not to increase the angle covered by your cast, just tilt the same angle backward or forward.

On short- and medium-distance casts, I believe it helps to think of the intended cast direction, your *target line,* as the direction you straighten the fly line at the end

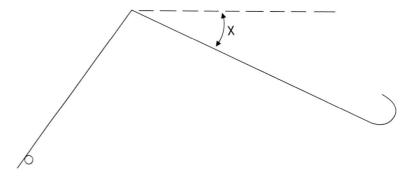

Figure 3-4. Measuring up/down tilt.

of a false cast—a foot or so above the water. On a twenty-foot cast, this target line may be angled downward from the rod tip thirty degrees or more below horizontal (figure 3-4). This intended direction approaches horizontal as you lengthen the cast. On your longest casts, the target line or initial trajectory is no longer equivalent to a false cast but is raised from the water for maximum line carry, often ten to twenty degrees above horizontal.

So, at times you need to be able to tilt your cast either forward (to lower the cast) or back (to raise the cast), and as you do, your casting hand also moves in a different direction. On a twenty-foot cast my fly line is angled downward from horizontal enough that my casting hand moves almost directly downward—then directly upward on the back cast. Yet during long upward-angled forward casts, your casting hand moves more forward than downward, much closer to horizontal (figure 3-5). So, contrary to some early writing, a caster's hand does not move parallel to the path of the rod tip but is somewhat offset in direction.

I emphasize lowering and raising the target line in my teaching because so many casters move the rod and fly line back and forth haphazardly. They grasp the importance of straightening the fly line, but not of straightening it in a particular direction. Typically they straighten the line too high in front, which invites dropping it too low in back. Starting with a very short cast forces you to aim downward, rather than straight ahead, which helps you pay attention to the direction of your cast.

Rod speed. This is the movement you vary in this book to change rod bend. Although speed is most important at the tip of the rod, you will work on varying the speed of your casting hand. When you add the *line hand* (i.e., the non-casting hand) in hauling, you vary the speed there as well. When casting a short line, there is no need to speed up your hand movement. Your purpose is line control, and you move the rod slowly enough to feel the rod's flexing.

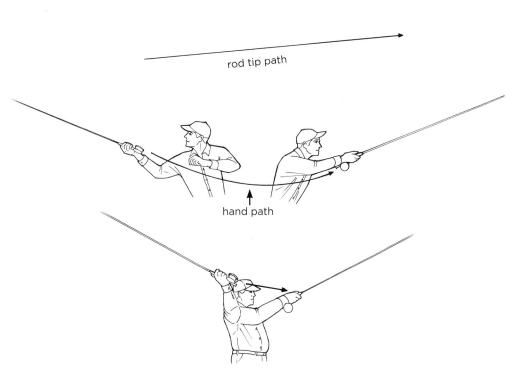

rod tip path

hand path

Figure 3-5. Hand/rod tip direction offset on a long cast.

Try to move your hand at the same speed, whether fast or slow, throughout the cast. Some authors have talked about accelerating the hand movement throughout the cast, as in *accelerating to a stop*. However, frame-by-frame analysis of various casters' movements has consistently shown that, after an initial acceleration to overcome inertia, a distance caster's hand accelerates a relatively small amount throughout the cast. Where most of the acceleration is occurring is at the rod's tip due to increased angular rotation and abrupt stopping and straightening of a bent lever. This acceleration of the tip continues well into the rod's straightening during its unloading.

Now you have been introduced to the four primary rod variables you will use to alter the path of your rod tip and fly line. I have illustrated how each one contributes to the efficiency of a short cast. Minimizing the stroke length and angular rotation allows you to concentrate the movement into the top two or three feet of the rod. Tilting the cast downward in front and up in back straightens the short line a foot or two above the water, and moving your rod slowly provides control and sufficient line speed.

In the next chapter I lay out my teaching progression for practicing this short overhead cast. I encourage you to try to work through these practices, even if the style is different from what you are accustomed to. Sometimes you can improve your cast by trying to do something in a different way. Even if you prefer to stay with your own style, you may at least benefit by shortening your stroke to eliminate wasted motion. This book is not as much about changing your style as it is about learning to adjust your fly rod's movement with whatever style you prefer.

CHAPTER 4

PRACTICE PROGRESSIONS FOR THE SHORT OVERHEAD CAST

When helping an experienced fly fisher, I can be laid back and accepting of differences in style. That person already has a casting style. However, when introducing a basic cast to someone, I need to start with the style I believe works best for most people. Beginning students often do not have a cast: habits have not yet been formed. And you are working with a skill in which a person's most common natural tendency—a loose wrist movement—interferes with success.

With a basic cast, I introduce the movements I believe are most helpful and keep tight control over the practice sessions—to prevent that natural wristiness from occurring before better habits have been formed. I know that somewhere in the learning I will have to give up on my style with certain students, but only after watching them struggle with it for a while. Some get it with a little persistence.

For now, I want you to become that beginning student and try to follow the practice sequence offered here. In doing so, you may find some wasted motion in your short cast or even pick up a movement that adds something you like better than what you have been doing.

1

Lowering your arm to the side allows you to watch the straight-line physics of your cast: (1) the fly line straightening behind the rod's tip, (2) the rod tip pulling the fly line forward along a straight path, and (3) the rod tip stopping to continue the efficient unrolling of a small loop and straightening of line. (See p. 40 for steps 2 and 3.)

2

3

PRACTICE #1: CASTING ARM ONLY

One way I try to guide a student's basic casting movements is to limit the initial practice to a single joint of the body—the shoulder joint, rather than the wrist or elbow joints that most people would naturally use. I don't do this to make life difficult, but to initially focus the practice on the single movement that I believe provides the best foundation for an overhead cast. This movement is easier to learn if emphasized through such isolated practice at the outset of the learning.

To emphasize this movement, I initially remove as many distractions as possible—the water or casting field, the fly line, and even the fly rod. I want your complete attention focused on learning to move your shoulder, so I have you practice with just your arm—substituting a pen for your fly rod. If you don't already have a grip you like, put your thumb on top with the index "trigger" finger opposite it. In this first practice, start with the simple arm motion of a short false cast without the extra

A pen can be your fly rod when practicing "shoulder isolation" movements.

movements of picking the line up off the water or laying it down again.

A preparatory position and movement. To start this practice, position the elbow of your casting arm to barely touch the side of your body. With your hand in front of you, grasp the pen and slowly bend your elbow until you have raised your pen-holding hand to chest level. Your forearm should now be in contact with your upper arm.

The back-cast movement. From this starting position, make your back-cast motion by using only your shoulder joint. Lift your hand and pen upward until your forearm is nearly vertical. This should raise your hand to about chin level. If you have done this short movement correctly, your elbow has left the side of your body in a forward and upward direction. (Moving your elbow forward in this way is called *shoulder flexion*.) With no movements taking place at the wrist or elbow joints, your

Start this shoulder practice with your casting hand at chest level.

forearm should still be in contact with your upper arm. The part of your pen that extends beyond your hand should now be pointing upward, about twenty degrees back from vertical. Your entire arm has been lifted. The word I use to guide this back-cast movement is *lift*.

The forward cast movement. To make the forward cast motion, *drop* or lower your arm to the starting position again with your hand back at chest level. Your elbow should have moved down and back to retouch the side of your body. (Moving your elbow back and down in this way from the shoulder is called *shoulder extension*.) In the absence of wrist movement, your pen should still be pointing upward, just slightly forward of vertical, and your upper arm should still be touching your lower arm. As your arm rotates about your shoulder in this way, your hand moves upward on the back cast, then downward on the forward cast—rather than backward and forward as you might have done before. Use a large

Back cast: Use only shoulder movement to lift your hand to chin level, and stop when your forearm reaches vertical.

Forward cast: Using only shoulder movement, return your hand to chest level. Holding a Nerf football (or some other similar object) at the elbow during these movements prevents any elbow straightening that would distract from the feel of shoulder movement.

mirror to compare your arm and hand positions to these photographs.

What to look for. Slowly repeat these up-and-down movements, keeping your mind coming back to your shoulder to be sure the movement hasn't shifted to other parts of your arm. If one of my students starts extending the elbow, I place a velcro-covered Nerf ball (i.e., six-inch-diameter ball) in that student's elbow joint, closing it until the forearm and upper arm together hold the ball in place throughout the movement. That prevents the elbow from moving and allows the student to feel the isolated shoulder movement. Also, make sure you are not moving too far by stopping your *lift* as your forearm approaches vertical and your *drop* as your hand reaches chest level.

When you believe you are doing these short, slow movements well, do them faster, making an abrupt stop of both the lift and drop movements by squeezing or tightening your fingers.

PRACTICE #2: ADDING THE FLY ROD

The purpose of this second practice is to get the feel of the rod's unloading as you stop the movement. You continue doing the same shoulder movement, but with your fly rod rather than your pen. However, do not string up the fly line yet. Most people underpower the back cast—so move the rod with enough speed during the lift to feel the rod bounce back or recoil against your hand as you stop abruptly. You should feel the rod's tip bounce again as you stop your forward casting motion at chest level. This practice allows you to continue to work on an isolated shoulder movement while adding the feel of the rod's unloading.

PRACTICE #3: ADDING THE FLY LINE

Adding the fly line allows you to watch how this movement is working. At this point you need to find a grass field for your practice. If there is a breeze, turn to let it hit you from your non-casting side—your left side, if casting right handed. Your fly line should be light colored or bright enough to be easily seen, the size to match your fly rod, and either a weight-forward or double-tapered design. For basic casting practice I recommend a 7 ½-foot 2X knotless-tapered leader and small tuft of yarn, about ½ inch across.

After stringing your rod, strip just enough line off your reel to be able to make a twenty-foot cast—only twelve feet of fly line plus the leader beyond your rod tip. You are practicing the short cast discussed in chapter 3. Start this practice with your fly line straight on the grass in front of you with your rod tip held within an inch of the ground. Use only your casting or *rod hand,* trapping the fly line against the cork grip with a finger to keep it from flopping around or pulling additional line off the reel. You add your non-casting or *line hand* later, when you no longer need to think as much about what your rod hand and arm are doing.

The casting movement. You start with a movement that is similar to what you did when first grasping your pen. Bend your elbow slowly until your hand reaches chest level. In doing this, you are raising the rod tip and watching your yarn fly slowly skip toward you along the grass. As your casting hand approaches chest level, speed up to make the back cast you have been practicing with shoulder movement. When you sense that the fly line is straightening behind you, start your forward cast by lowering your arm and hand to chest level again. As your line straightens in the air in front of you, start another back cast. Make a series of five to ten of these false casts before lowering your hand and rod to let the line fall to the grass.

Picking the line up off the grass and laying it down again are not my main concern here. I want you to think about the shoulder movement that is occurring during your false casting. With each series of false casts, ask yourself one of these three questions: Am I using only the shoulder joint as I practiced? Am I stopping my *lift* when my forearm reaches vertical and stopping my forward cast when my hand reaches chest level? Is my casting hand moving up and down, rather than backward and forward? Without seeing your first few casts, I would bet that you have suddenly found yourself adding extra arm or wrist movements. If so, adjust again to make these casts with only shoulder movement. The more you can rely on the strong muscles of the shoulder to drive the fly line forward, the more distance you will eventually be able to cast before adding other parts of your body. Although this isolation exercise can be important in establishing a basic casting movement, you will need to add another movement to it to achieve tight casting loops.

PRACTICE #4: ADDING TIP CASTING

In this practice you emphasize using the tip of your fly rod. You still have only twelve feet of fly line beyond that tip. Start by opening up your stance (i.e., dropping your casting side back) to be able to turn your head upward to watch your rod tip as you cast. As you false cast this short line back and forth, try to limit the bending to the top two feet of your rod. To do this, move the rod just far enough to see a little bending—then stop your cast. Remember, you are looking up at that tip *throughout* the cast to see where the bend is occurring. As the line unrolls over the tip of your rod and begins to straighten, start moving the rod back the other direction. When you see your rod start to bend, stop again. If you can make these short false casts by stopping the butt soon enough to keep the flexing in the tip, tiny casting loops that barely clear your rod tip should form in both directions. (If your line hits the rod tip on the forward cast, lower your forward hand movement just enough to get the rod tip out of the way.) The error I expect to see in your practice is waving the rod's butt back and forth too far. With so little line beyond the rod tip, your rod butt might only move one clock position—from eleven to twelve o'clock, certainly no more than two clock positions. Remember, you need to limit butt movement to emphasize tip movement.

Sometimes, when you open up your stance and turn your head upward, you lose control over the way your arm moves. So as soon as you are tip casting successfully on both the back cast and the forward cast, return to your squared stance and shoulder movement. But, as you do, continue to stop your rod to emphasize tip movement. Your casting loops may now look smaller than ever before. If you close your eyes, you should be able to feel the tip of your fly rod working.

PRACTICE #5: ADDING THE FINAL ACCELERATION

This practice adds final tip speed to your short forward cast. To do this, try to get your fly to land first, before the leader and fly line. Having the fly land first provides a visual test of your ability to speed up your rod's tip late in the forward cast. To get your fly to hit first with 12 feet of fly line and a 7½-foot leader beyond the tip, tilt your forward false cast lower by stopping your back cast high—when your rod butt reaches vertical. You also need to stop your hand at chest level on the forward cast. If your fly is still not landing first, start pressing with your thumb *as you stop the rod.* As mentioned earlier, this thumb press adds a slight, quick wrist pivot to your stop. This is the first practice in which you have added something to your shoulder movement—a late wrist movement. This additional movement should tighten up your casting loops.

Look up at the tip to see when to stop the rod early enough to see just the tip bending (left) and the unrolling of a tiny loop (right).

PRACTICE #6: PICK UP AND LAY DOWN—A PART METHOD

Sometimes, even in such short-line practice, it helps to simplify movement by making only the back cast, then only the forward cast. This is especially true when—in the absence of an instructor—you are learning a movement from written instructions.

To do this, slowly lift your hand to chest level before speeding up to make your back cast *lift*. Your fly line should fall to the grass behind you. Move forward a step or two to get rid of any slack in this fallen line. Use this moment to check your arm position for making your forward cast: forearm vertical, upper arm in contact with forearm, hand at chin level. Then make your forward cast by lowering your hand to chest level and pressing with your thumb. Did the fly land first? If not, you have probably lowered your hand too far or pressed too early with your thumb. If you let your hand drop below chest level, you also lower the rod tip too far, which invites

the fly line closest to you to land first. If you press your thumb early or aim your forward cast too high, your fly kicks over too high in the air and the fly line will again land first. Remember to angle your cast downward in front, stop your hand at chest level, and delay the thumb press until you are stopping the rod. You are learning the sequence of starting your shoulder movement before adding your wrist, which is important.

In these instructions, I have introduced one casting style. I like this style because it invites delicacy in a short cast yet builds in strength for an effective long cast. Sometimes I find myself scrambling up small mountain streams with a fly rod in one hand and a wading staff in the other. I am fishing a dry fly there by doing exactly what I have taught here—using one hand to cast tiny loops off the tip. At other times I find myself wading on saltwater flats, using this strong shoulder movement to drive heavy lines into the wind.

Although casting only twenty feet here, you have been learning a shoulder movement that should enable you to make a forty- to fifty-foot cast—before even adding the line hand and elbow movements that will further increase the distance. If you try saltwater fly fishing armed with only a wrist- or elbow-dominated casting motion, saltwater guides are likely to criticize your weak trout cast in much the same tone that trout guides sometimes criticize the bull-in-the-china-shop casting movements of some saltwater anglers. Today's fly fisher should be able to excel both with short tip casts and strong wind casts.

I hope you try these practices. But even if you are not comfortable with the movement style I have taught here, I hope you have picked up something that keeps you from wasting motion. The arm movements you use to make short casts should include a high-to-low forward hand movement to aim the fly line downward. These should be short, firm movements with little angle change to get the most out of your rod's tip. And you should use some type of shoulder movement to start the line going forward smoothly.

CHAPTER 5

ADDING THE LINE HAND

When I want to concentrate on the feel of a fly rod, I often cast using only my rod hand. Yet we typically use both hands when fly fishing. Adding the line hand to a false cast adds technique, and with it, the possibility of other casting errors. So, improving your basic cast includes line-hand as well as rod-hand techniques. But before delving into the line hand further, I want to say more about false casting.

FALSE CASTING

You are false casting whenever you cast the fly line back and forth in the air without letting it fall to the water. It is *false,* or at least incomplete, in that it is not allowed to drop to do real fishing. Most instructors teach a pick-up-and-lay-down cast first, having you lift the line off the grass or water with each back cast and lay it down again with each forward cast. When switching to false casting, the initial back cast and forward cast are the same until the leader straightens in the air in front. Then you start your next back cast, rather than letting your line fall to the water.

Uses. Most fly casters start using a false cast to increase distance. On a trout stream, you soon learn a second use—shaking water from the hackles of a dry fly to improve its float. The third use, changing direction, may occur to you suddenly on a lake when, in the middle of a cast, a fish rises off to one side. Rotating your upper body helps change the direction of the next false casts to drop the fly near that rise.

There is another important use of the false cast that is sometimes overlooked: making corrections. This includes fine-tuning the distance or direction of the cast for accuracy, raising or lowering your target line, or changing your timing, rod angle, stroke length, force, or rod bend. You often make these corrections to improve the size or shape of your casting loop. You will be using the false cast in this way in other practices I introduce.

False casting can become so much of your practice that you begin to overdo it when fishing. Guides sometimes have to remind their clients that, "The fish are in the water, not in the sky." The number of false casts is even more critical in bonefishing, where one too many will spook an approaching fish. Experienced Bahamian guides say, "Drop it, Mon," which can be interpreted to mean, "Let that cast fall to the water. Do *not* make another false cast." With such help, you soon learn to fish with as few false casts as necessary.

Ultimately, you learn to regard the false cast as part of your approach to wary fish. So you extend line well off to the side, often with a low, sidearm motion; or, lacking a choice of casting angles, you false cast short of the fish, extending line only on the final delivery. Both quick rod movements and line flash spook fish when false casting. Although you sometimes need to false cast line out quickly ahead of a moving bonefish, you learn to do so with as slow and deliberate a rod movement as time permits. Moving the rod slowly to get line out quickly presents an intriguing study in the efficiency of movement.

THE LINE HAND

Holding the line to prevent slack. When casting with your rod hand only, you controlled your line by trapping it against the cork grip. This prevented additional line from creeping off the reel. Yet the need to change casting distance calls for a better way to control the release of that line. Placing the line in your non-casting hand gives you a way to do that. Although you eventually use this line hand to shoot, retrieve, and haul line, you first train it to hold the line in a way that prevents slack. You might think of slack beyond the rod tip, but here you are concerned with slack that forms between your line hand and the stripping guide of your rod (the first guide up from your reel). This slack will occur if your line hand and rod hand move toward each other as you apply force to your forward cast. Such slack can work up the rod and interfere with how it bends and transfers energy to the fly line. I often see this subtle line-hand error in the technique of otherwise skilled fly fishers.

Some casting teachers try to prevent this slack by having students move the line hand in relation to the rod hand: up and back on the back cast, and down and forward on the forward cast, avoiding slack by keeping the hands the same distance apart. They believe that holding the line hand stationary creates slack during the forward cast when the rod hand approaches it.

Yet I have found that moving the line hand gives some students too much to think about. They begin to lose what they have been working on with the rod hand. Some start moving the line hand farther than the rod hand without realizing it, causing the line hand to approach the stripping guide during the back cast. This creates the same slack in the back cast that you started moving your line hand to prevent in the forward cast.

I prefer that students hold the line hand stationary (for simplicity) but far enough to the side so the two hands do not approach one another. Holding the line close to your front pants pocket (on the line-hand side) keeps that line hand approximately the same distance from the stripping guide throughout the casting movement (figure 5-1). When you learn the double haul, your well-timed hauls or pulls with the line hand will further increase the tension on that line.

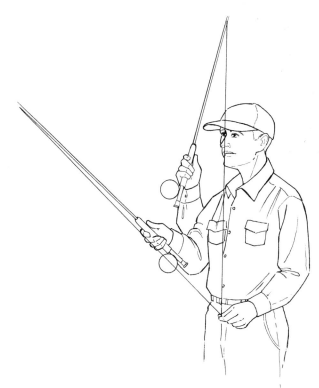

Figure 5-1. Line hand positioned to maintain tension up to the stripping guide throughout the cast.

Shooting line into the cast. To add casting distance, you need to know when and how to release additional line into the cast. This is called *shooting line.* So far, you have been holding it between your thumb and forefinger throughout the cast. To shoot line, you first need to make sure that line is available by pulling or *stripping* it off your reel and letting it fall to the ground. Slack there is not a problem, because your line hand prevents it from moving up the rod until needed. Then, as you are false casting, you release the line through your line hand when you have stopped a forward cast and see your casting loop form in the air. After shooting this line into the cast, you may have trouble grabbing it again in time to start fishing effectively. To avoid such mishandling of line, release it from your thumb and forefinger to the inside, or palm side, of those fingers (figure 5-2). When you immediately rejoin the tips of the thumb and forefinger, they should be encircling, but not holding that moving fly line. The line is free to move, but under

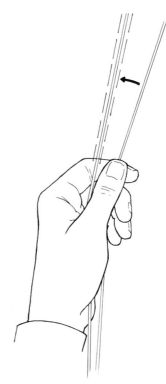

Figure 5-2. Shooting line by releasing it into the control of your hand.

constant control. Whenever you want to stop the line's movement up through the rod, just close your fingers on it.

I add these new parts to the cast in three stages. The first stage is already in place, because you were false casting with your rod hand when practicing short casts. Here you add another twelve feet of fly line beyond the rod to the twelve feet you were casting then. With the leader and some rod length, you should now be landing your fly thirty to thirty-five feet from where you stand—what I think of as an average trout cast. These practices progress from false casting with the rod hand, to adding the line hand, and finally to shooting line.

PRACTICE #7: ADDING FLY LINE TO YOUR FALSE CAST

The only new thing here is the addition of the twelve feet of fly line, which means you now have twenty-four feet of fly line and the leader beyond the tip. As you attempt casting this additional line with only the rod hand, you should first notice that your forward casts may now be ticking the ground in front. To cast this extra line well, you need to raise your target line by tilting your rod stops back a little. Twelve additional feet of fly line has also added some weight to your cast, which bends the rod a little more. This means you need to widen the angle through which your rod moves to keep the rod tip moving along a straight path.

One way to see this difference for yourself is to practice early or late enough on a sunny day that you can watch your shadow in front of you as you cast. Sometimes I have students make a few casts at this distance—watching their rod's shadow. Then I have them strip in the additional twelve feet of fly line and watch again. As you watch, you should see changes in the rod's tilt, angle of rotation, and bend. Even as these changes begin to occur, try to keep your stroke length short and emphasize shoulder movement. If you need more force, try raising your rod hand a little higher on the back cast rather than extending your arm movement forward.

PRACTICE #8: ADDING THE LINE HAND

As you add your line hand, emphasize your new hand position off to the side. If you cast right-handed, hold your line in your left hand, about six inches in front of your left front pants pocket. In this part of your false-cast practice, try to feel constant line tension up to the stripping guide throughout the cast. If you notice your line hand moving a little during the cast to maintain tension, that's fine. You are focusing on the most important thing.

PRACTICE #9: SHOOTING THE LINE

Next add the release of additional line and combine these elements into what I call an *upstream fishing presentation*. If you haven't done this before, you are casting different amounts of fly line in the same series of casts

Returning line control to your rod hand for fishing.

and learning that your timing changes as your casting distance changes. You need to allow more time to complete a longer cast. You are also learning to transfer the control of the line from your line hand when casting, to your rod hand when stripping line back in. I teach casting with your *hands apart* and fishing with your *hands together*. In this practice, I also teach fishing with the rod tip low and have students set the hook on command by separating the line and rod hands enough to quickly move the fly a few inches on the grass or water. In this technique, I teach setting the hook by moving the rod hand up and away as the line hand moves down and away to the opposite side. For now, your focus is on the casting technique.

Start this practice by stripping off yet another twelve feet of fly line, which now gives you thirty-six feet of fly line beyond the rod's tip. Strip in—but don't reel in—most of that line to start your false casting. Release six to twelve inches of that line into each forward false cast before pinching the line again. If the line doesn't shoot easily through the rod, you are probably releasing it too early, before enough weight is out in front to help pull more line through the rod. Make sure you have stopped the forward cast before releasing that line. As the final cast is straightening and falling to the grass or water, bring your line hand directly across to the rod, hooking the line on the partially open index finger (or second finger if you prefer) of your rod hand. With the rod tip lowered, strip the line back in on the water or grass with your line hand from behind the rod hand's control point—as if keeping pace with a current that brings the fly downstream toward you. When you have stripped in most of the fly line, separate your hands again and gently lift the rod into a back cast to start the next cycle of false casting.

This is the point in my practice progressions where I believe a beginning student has learned enough to start fishing. I believe many of the people who become frustrated with fly fishing have not practiced in these ways before going to the stream. Before going, you should also read up on other dimensions of the sport, particularly wading safety and angler etiquette.

PRACTICE #10: ADDING THE ELBOW

With the thirty-six feet of fly line plus the leader beyond the rod tip, you may be making casts of forty-five to fifty feet. Try casting this much line with just your rod hand, using only your shoulder movement and thumb press. If you lack the strength to cast this much line well with your short casting movement, lengthen your casting stroke by adding a little elbow movement. I believe it is good practice to cast as much line as possible with a short, simple stroke and add elbow extension only when you need more strength. Eventually, each of us finds a point at which we need the help from a longer stroke. You are starting to make a transition to distance casting.

Part II

BETTER DISTANCE CAST

CHAPTER 6

CASTING FOR DISTANCE: PURPOSE CHANGES MOVEMENTS

"What's the point of casting so far? Most trout are caught within thirty-five feet." This may be your thought after watching people unleash their longest casts at a fishing show. If you fish only in small, narrow trout streams, who can argue? But many of today's fly fishers also enjoy taking their sport to lakes, wide rivers, and saltwater flats, where long casts reach more fish. Bonefishing guides have confirmed my impression that only about half of the fish they see taken on a fly are caught on casts of thirty-five feet or less. Being able to throw sixty-foot casts can make your day. And I have cast to steelhead and salmon tightly grouped on the far side of rivers that required a seventy-five-foot cast. When you back off from attempting ninety-foot casts, a sixty-foot cast can feel almost effortless. So pushing your cast to its outer limits—whatever that is—can not only get you into additional fish: it also makes shorter casts easier.

Although the basic overhead cast forms the foundation for your distance cast, enough things change that a long cast sometimes seems like a different skill. And, even when we concentrate only on long casts, people have different ways of moving. It is not always clear what you should change or try to keep the same.

Each purpose has its own demands. In an earlier chapter, you were introduced to the idea that casters move differently and that some of these differences are due to changing the purpose of the cast. This should not be surprising because each purpose has somewhat different demands or guiding principles. For example, accuracy depends on consistency—being able to hit a target repeatedly. Consistency, in turn, benefits from simplicity. If you can keep a movement simple, you stand the best chance of repeating it exactly. There are fewer things that can go wrong. So it makes sense that biomechanical principles such as shortening your casting motion, moving fewer body parts, and slowing your muscular action would guide this movement.

On the other hand, casting as far as possible depends on your ability to use additional force and generate speed in your movement. So it makes sense to follow principles such as lengthening your casting motion, using additional body movements, and speeding up your muscular contraction. If you change your casting purpose from short-line accuracy to maximum distance, you sometimes rely on the opposite principles and movements to be effective.

Efficiency of a long cast. Adding parts to a long cast and speeding up the timing increase the demand on your coordination. In this sense, a long cast is a more athletic skill than a short cast. These extra movements also affect your approach to efficiency. When casting short, you tried to eliminate extra movements to use as few parts as possible. When casting long, you add parts. Efficiency is now viewed as adding as many parts as it takes to accomplish a task that is more difficult.

We apply this additive approach to efficiency even with a basic cast when teaching children. Their lack of arm strength adds to the difficulty and may be countered by using long movements; short, light rods; and even casting with two hands.

So the change from short to long casts provides a clear picture of how changing your purpose also changes your movements. This was confirmed to me during a follow-up study Dr. Gary Moran and I conducted in January 1997. In that study, we filmed seven outstanding casters, including Lefty Kreh, Jerry Siem, Bruce Richards, and George Cook. We intentionally selected casters with very different casting styles and had each one make the same casts with the identical fly rods and lines. We were primarily interested in looking at similarities and differences in the movements of world-class casters by changing only one thing at a time. For example, in one comparison we kept the fly line and casting distance the same, changing only the fly rod being used: full flex versus tip flex. In another comparison, we used the same fly rod to make long casts but with different types of fly line: shooting taper versus weight-forward. Finally we kept the rod and fly line the same but changed the distance of the cast: short cast for accuracy versus long cast. This last comparison revealed much greater differences in movements than did the other two.

DIFFERENCES BETWEEN THE MOVEMENTS OF SHORT AND LONG CASTS

In this comparison, a thirty-five-foot cast to a target was contrasted to a distance cast of approximately ninety feet. We found that each of these casters, regardless of their casting style, made the same five changes or adjustments to meet the added demands of distance. They bent the rod more, added stroke length, angular rotation and speed, and tilted the cast upward.

The first difference that drew my attention was rod bend. I had known from our initial study that the fly rod bends its deepest just as your rod hand stops the cast. I also knew that the additional line weight and force required to make a long cast would deepen the bend in the rod. But, even with this knowledge, I was startled by how much the rod bent in a ninety-foot cast as compared to a thirty-five-foot cast (figure 6-1). The comparison in this illustration points out a second change or adjustment to a long cast—changing the downward-angled target direction of a short forward cast to an upward-angled target direction on the long forward cast. Up/down rod tilt changes impressively with distance.

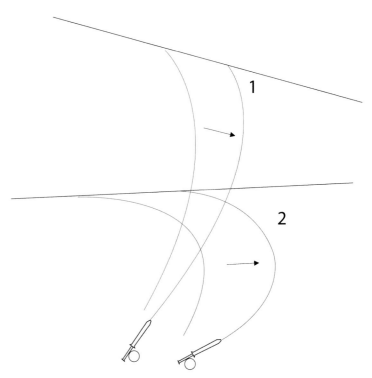

Figure 6-1. Rod bend and up/down tilt differences between (1) 35-foot and (2) 90-foot casts.

When the fly rod bends deeply during a long cast, its tip also drops much lower than when casting short. To move that lowered tip through a straight path, you also need to lower it at the start and end of the cast. This is done by widening the rod's angular rotation until the tip is lowered to match the amount of bend. (When discuss-ing a short cast in chapter 3, we intentionally kept the angular rotation narrow to emphasize movement in the rod's tip.) The seven expert casters in this study rotated the rod butt forward an average of 133 degrees during the long casts as contrasted to only 78 degrees during the shorter, thirty-five-foot casts (figure 6-2).

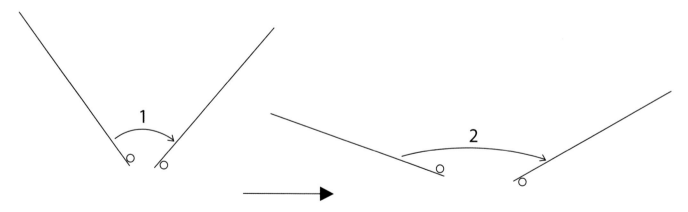

Figure 6-2. Angular rotation in (1) 35-foot and (2) 90-foot casts.

This comparison of short to long casts also allowed us to study differences in stroke length—the distance the hand moves the rod butt toward the target during the cast. We found that all seven experts, when changing from short to long casts, changed both the direction and distance that their casting hand moved. The hand movements during the forward stroke of the thirty-five-foot cast were short and more downward than forward. During the long cast, the hand movements were much longer and directed more forward than downward—much closer to horizontal. Lefty Kreh's stroke length for a long cast was eighty-four inches or seven feet. Interestingly, his stroke length for the

Figure 6-3. Stroke length and angular rotation differences between Lefty's (1) 35-foot and (2) 90-foot casts.

thirty-five-foot cast was only seven inches forward (figure 6-3). Although the differences in Lefty's movements were more extreme than most, such differences were found in each expert's casts—which confirms the teaching concept, "short cast, short stroke; long cast, long stroke."

Although our study was not set up to measure speed of the casts, frame-by-frame analysis did show that each caster moved the rod and casting hand faster through the longer movement of the distance cast than through the shorter movement of the thirty-five-foot cast.

So each caster in our study, when switching from short to long casts, rotated the fly rod through wider angles, bent the rod more, moved the casting hand farther, aimed the forward cast higher, and increased the speed of both the casting and hauling hand. These adjustments are accounted for in the four primary rod variables you learn to adjust in this book.

How do you add these different movements to your basic cast? You have already taken an important first step

When casting short, the movements of the fly rod, including rod angle, stroke length, speed, and bend, are minimized for efficient line flow.

by working on conserving energy in the movements of your short cast. By identifying and eliminating wasted force and rod movement, you have made these movements available to help provide additional force to your long casts. The additional movements need to be added carefully. Years of teaching have taught me that most people have trouble learning more than one new thing at a time. So I have developed a practice sequence for making these changes to a distance cast.

PRACTICE #11: INCREASING STROKE LENGTH

For the next three practices, strip out enough line to land the fly about sixty feet from where you stand. This is enough distance to let you experiment with additional movements without being tempted to throw the line as far as you can. As you do this, practice increasing your stroke length first. Start by opening up your stance to invite a longer movement and begin casting. Add to your

stroke length first by moving your body—shifting your weight back on the back cast and forward to start the forward cast. Shifting your weight as you lean back and forth also provides a little rhythm that can help your timing. When this additional body movement feels comfortable, add even more stroke length by reaching your casting hand back farther on the back cast and forward on the forward cast.

PRACTICE #12: RAISING THE TARGET LINE

When you feel comfortable with a longer stroke, start aiming your forward cast higher. Make this change in your up/down tilt by stopping your rod farther back (lower) on your back cast and higher on your forward cast. As a right-handed caster you may also bend your right knee during the low back cast and straighten it again during the forward weight shift to help lift the forward cast upward. *Drifting* the rod tip into a lower angle after the back cast, as will be taught later, also helps angle the forward cast upward. After stopping your cast, try to hold the rod at an angle that allows the fly line to shoot through the rod guides easily.

PRACTICE #13: WIDENING THE ROD'S ANGLE OF ROTATION AND ADDING SPEED

After adding stroke length and raising your point of aim, consciously start widening the angle your rod rotates through. Again adjust your back-cast stop a little farther back, but also let your forward cast continue farther to a lower stop point as well. As mentioned, this wider angle allows you to keep the tip moving in a straight path as you add speed and deepen the rod's bend.

I will talk more about speed when introducing the *double haul.* Before adding the final pieces to our distance cast, I want to add something more about different styles that become noticeable when people add force and movements for distance casting.

CHAPTER 7

STYLE DIFFERENCES IN DISTANCE CASTING

Casters move differently from one another, even when their purpose is the same. These differences become most noticeable when extra movements have been added to attempt a distance cast. Differences often come from your physical characteristics or individual movement tendencies. For example, a tall person may cast farther than a shorter person because longer levers moved at a given speed produce greater tip speed than shorter levers. Yet the shorter person sometimes casts longer by possessing the strength or arm speed to move the lever system faster than the taller person. People begin to rely on different movement patterns to gain an advantage, sometimes without knowing why.

ARM STYLES

In studying expert casters, I have been surprised by how many different ways people can vary the hand and arm movements to cast. I believe that how you use the casting arm is the most distinctive element of style in a fly cast. As a first step in attempting to describe such differences, I have lumped them into three general styles, recognized by how the elbow is positioned at the start of the forward cast: forward, up to the side, or low. These positions set the stage for movement differences that have more to do with the shoulder than the elbow. The elbow is a simple hinge joint that can only open (extend) or close (flex). The shoulder, however, is a ball-and-socket joint that allows the arm to apply force in a variety of ways. This is where most arm differences occur. Understanding vari-

ous types of arm movement allows you to view your own casting stroke in relation to several existing styles. As I describe these styles, you might want to imitate them to see which style best describes your cast. You might also benefit in some way from experimenting with the feel of a different style.

Elbow-forward style. The movements I start a beginning class with lead to what I have called the *elbow-forward style.* At the start of the forward cast, your elbow is below your hand and somewhat forward of your casting shoulder.

Positioning your elbow forward of your shoulder gives you the potential to add forceful elbow extension to your forward cast. This is an abbreviated version of an overhand ball throw, a movement sometimes referred to as a *kinetic whip.* This name refers to the fact that each part—the shoulder, elbow, and wrist—move in a whip-like sequence, each adding something to the overall force. In a cast, the rod tip continues that whip-like sequence when you stop the rod's butt. I introduce this movement by teaching the shoulder movement first, then add the wrist by pressing the thumb, and finally add the elbow to help your distance cast.

This upright forearm is also important to accuracy by leading and controlling the vertical forward movement of your fly rod and unrolling fly line. I believe this is why most tournament casters use an elbow-forward style. Among the elbow-forward casters who benefited from tournament casting are Jimmy Green, Mel Krieger, Steve and Tim Rajeff, and Joan Wulff. Bill Cairns, Jerry Siem, and Gary Borger also cast with an elbow-forward style.

"Elbow-forward" arm style.

Elbow-up-to-the-side style. In what I call the *elbow-up-to-the-side style,* the forward cast starts with your elbow positioned directly out to your side at about shoulder level with your casting hand directly above your elbow. If, from this position, your elbow came forward first, I would classify it as an elbow-forward cast. However, if the hand leads the elbow forward from that position, I consider it to be an elbow-up-to-the-side style. In this style, the upper arm acts like a rotisserie, rotating without going anywhere. Thus, on your back cast, your forearm and rod are rotated up and backward around a stationary elbow and then rotated *ahead of your elbow* on your

"Elbow-up-to-the-side" arm style.

forward cast. (This shoulder movement is called *external rotation* on the back cast and *internal rotation* coming forward.) Casting instructors sometimes criticize this arm style as being a poor throwing motion because your elbow lags behind your hand. However, the shoulder part of the movement, so important to this style, *is* similar to that used in a ball throw.

I most often see this style in people who are casting while wading deep or from a float tube, where the need exists to keep the elbow high and dry. I also see this style used by stream anglers who cast nymph riggings with weight on the leader. To avoid tangling, they use wide loops and change the casting plane, making a sidearm back cast, then lifting the elbow to come forward over the top. If you use a certain arm movement enough in your fishing, it can creep into and change the way you cast in general. A number of fine casters, including Dan Blanton and Bruce Richards, cast beautiful loops with versions of this style.

Low-elbow style. In a baseball throw as well as in the two casting styles described thus far, your elbow is often raised to shoulder level. The upper arm forms approximately a ninety-degree angle with your body. In the *low-elbow style,* however, your elbow is kept much lower and closer to your body, typically moved back and forth from the shoulder. When casting for distance, most low-elbow casters use an open stance, a long arm movement, and a rod canted down somewhat from vertical. This arm style is well suited to the demands of saltwater fly fishing. The low arm and hand position provides additional strength to help you force a bend into stiff heavy fly rods, the long arm movement helps control long lines in the wind, and the sidearm cast helps keep heavy rods low and big hooks off to the side. In trout-fishing schools, I most often select this style to provide a strong arm position for small or slightly built students, as well as to teach a sidearm cast.

Chico Fernandez, the saltwater expert from Florida, provides a classic picture of a low-elbow style. Lefty Kreh

often casts with a low elbow, but brings it up close to shoulder level at times. Some anglers keep the elbow low on short casts, but raise it to cast farther. Other casters combine the movements of these distinctive styles in various ways. So my simple categories don't always hold up. However, they do offer a first step in understanding how casters benefit from using the casting arm in different ways.

Why do I make a big deal out of different casting styles? Aren't we overanalyzing something that is supposed to be fun? Maybe so, but information that can simplify your fishing movements and improve your casting skill may add to that

"Low-elbow" arm style.

fun. I believe that understanding styles can also help you appreciate your own cast. In the years I have been teaching and writing about casting styles, I have been surprised by the number of people who were relieved to find that it is OK to cast differently than their instructors. If your line flow and loops are good, you should not have to feel self-conscious.

So, some of us lift and lower the casting arm, some move it more back and forth, some rotate the forearm around a stationary upper arm, and others combine these movements. I suggest you rig up your fly rod and try to imitate each style. Where does your cast fit within these categories? You may find that you already adjust your elbow forward to present a fly accurately to a rising fish. You may also have been forced to keep your elbow high when attempting a long cast with water lapping at the top of your waders. And you may have lowered your arm to force additional bend into a stiff rod. I believe that most versatile fly fishers vary their basic casting strokes in response to fishing conditions such as these. Adaptation is important to successful fishing, even in the way you use your arm to cast.

USE OF THE BODY

You also see skilled distance casters using their body differently to provide additional force to the casting arm. Having played baseball competitively, I assumed you would get your best distance by dropping your casting (throwing) side back. I seem to recall that roughly 50 percent of your force in a baseball throw comes from your body and 50 percent from your ball-throwing arm. Apparently your body does not play as great a role in fly casting, perhaps due to the addition of a long, flexible lever with a tip that is restricted by having to move the fly line along a straight path. The result is an increased role for the caster's arm and fly rod and a reduced role for the body. Nevertheless, the body does make an important contribution.

A few years ago, Mel Krieger challenged me to try casting for distance with different stances. Although he taught an open stance for distance casting, he claimed he could personally cast as far with other stances. On the casting field the next morning I was surprised to find that I could cast virtually the same distance with either an open stance, squared stance, or closed stance. What I concluded was that each stance allows you to use your body in different ways to add about the same amount of force to your arm. The distance of my casts dropped off only when I eliminated any use of my body to help

When going for distance, efficiency means adding parts: lengthening the stroke, widening the rod angle, speeding up both rod and hauling movements, and raising your point of aim.

my casting arm. This experiment reinforced what I had found in my first research on distance casting. Our more successful elite distance casters used weight shift, body lean, and/or body rotation to help cast farther, whereas the less successful good casters more often attempted to provide force from the arm alone and generally did not cast as far.

In our second study we found some differences in the way casters used their body. Lefty Kreh's open stance, body lean, and long arm movement allowed him to use his entire body to apply force. George Cook achieved a long forward movement from a squared stance primarily by rotating his upper body. Jerry Siem applied force explosively with a more limited, but precisely timed shoulder movement (figure 7-1).

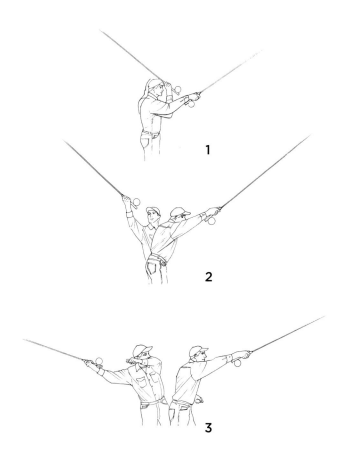

Figure 7-1. Body movement styles in distance casting: (1) shoulder only, (2) upper body rotation, and (3) full body lean.

In commenting on this difference, Lefty reminded me that Jerry is a big, powerful guy who can get away with a short movement for a long cast. I agree with Lefty that most people who cast long with a relatively short stroke are very strong in the shoulder area. Lefty's long stroke takes full advantage of his great coordination throughout his body and impressive forearm and hand strength. I believe it is important to experiment to find a movement style that matches your own strengths.

CHAPTER 8

ADDING DRIFT

In fly fishing, we are partial to the term *drift*. We speak of drifting a section of river, of our fly's drag-free drift, and of the drift of aquatic insects. There are those who might even regard some of us as drifters, for all the days we fish while moving from one river to the next. But the term drift also comes up in casting, usually to describe a movement added to the back cast when going for distance. This drift, after the force has been applied, was called *follow-through* as far back as 1942 in John Alden Knight's book, *Modern Fly Casting*.

Yet how can you consider making a follow-through movement when so much emphasis is placed on stopping the rod abruptly? How and when do you add drift to your casting movements and how does it help add distance to a cast? The answers to these questions could lead you to make a change in your cast that improves your loops and timing as well as adds to your distance.

What happens in drift? In a short overhead cast, you stop abruptly by physically stopping your casting hand and rod. When experts make long casts, however, their hand and rod butt sometimes keep moving without any noticeable pause between the back cast and forward cast. In studying film, I found this hand movement so smooth and continuous that the only way to tell when the back cast had ended was to look farther up the rod to see where it started to lose its bend. A cast sometimes ends with a deceleration rather than an obvious stop. Yet, even when your hand does not completely stop, you still experience the sensations of stopping and feeling the rod unload. So, apparently, an effective stop can occur, even though the rod continues to drift back.

Lefty Kreh provides a classic example of hand movement in drifting, sometimes moving his rod hand back nearly a foot and a half after his back cast begins unloading. Jerry Siem's drift opens up as much as forty degrees of additional rod angle for the next forward cast without any backward hand movement at all. This comparison of drift styles of two great casters made me realize that our concept of drift should not be limited to moving the casting hand back. Drift is not as much about the hand's additional movement as it is about the fly rod's additional movement—which can include drifting farther back or into a wider angle (figure 8-1).

As I continued to study the film of distance casters, I found that most of them drift the rod farther back *and* into a wider angle. So, as Lefty drifts his hand back,

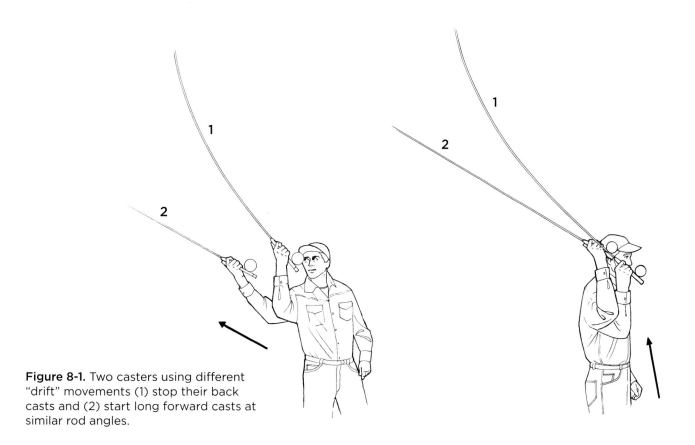

Figure 8-1. Two casters using different "drift" movements (1) stop their back casts and (2) start long forward casts at similar rod angles.

his rod tip also drops down to open up additional angle. When moving his hand forward again before applying force to his forward cast, he continues to lay his rod even farther back toward horizontal. At this point he almost appears to be carrying a javelin forward. In this way, his cast approaches the nine to three o'clock angle he has written about (figure 8-2).

But why drift at all? Why not make the entire backward movement in one motion, as you do when casting a short line? Some casters do just that when attempting a distance cast, but they usually find that their casting loops suffer. Why is that, and how can drift help?

Advantages of back-cast drift. Whether you slide your hand back, increase the rod angle, or combine the two, your drift is moving the rod tip back to set up a longer rod movement for the next forward cast. This longer tip path provides additional distance in which to generate speed and rod bend.

Figure 8-2. Rod positions during drift: (1) during the initial unloading of the back cast, (2) with angle opening and hand extended back, and (3) with angle opened almost to horizontal as hand is brought forward into position to start the forward cast.

Although you stop the back cast with the tip going upward, there are also some overlooked advantages to drifting the tip lower after that stop. Drifting the tip down in back widens the angle for the rod to rotate through, making it easier to put more bend in the rod yet keep the tip moving along a straight path. Dropping the rod tip low in back on the last back cast also helps set up an upward-angled forward tip path for the farthest line carry. If you try to lower your rod tip into this position on your back-cast movement without a drift, your tip will drop downward behind you in a way that pulls the fly line downward with it, resulting in big, ugly loops. I often see that in the long back casts of experienced anglers who have not learned to drift the rod.

Drift can also add speed to your cast. Some casters delay their drift movement until it almost seems to be part of the forward cast—a quick backward movement that continues into the forward cast. This backward drift movement is made as the caster shifts weight forward into the forward cast. This reminds me of a baseball hitter who is still moving his hands and bat back as he starts striding forward toward the pitcher. This timing results in continuous motion between the back cast and forward cast, which provides an early acceleration into the forward movement. The longest casts of Jerry Siem and Tim Rajeff provide great examples of this timing.

Drift also offers another advantage: keeping connected to your fly line and fly. When you first learn to cast, there is a separation between the back cast and forward cast—a slight pause when the rod is stopped in back and you momentarily lose the feeling of contact to the line. A little crosswind at that moment accentuates the feeling of that loss of contact. Yet if you drift the rod tip back a little with the flow of line after stopping the back cast, you can maintain enough tension to keep some feel to the fly line. A more obvious example of keeping connected with your line occurs when you change the casting plane from a sidearm back cast to an overhead forward cast without stopping your hand.

There is something else important that happens as the rod is drifting. When making a long back cast, some casters let their arm drift back to straighten behind them when following the rod tip back. Such arm reach during a rod's unloading can keep the tip moving with the layout of a long back-cast line, yet leaves you with a weak arm position for throwing the next forward cast. So, as the line continues to unroll in back, you take the opportunity to

After a long back cast, the casting arm (1) may be drifted backward, then (2) repositioned to a stronger position for the next forward cast.

1

2

reposition your casting arm forward into your strongest throwing position before applying force to the forward cast. Even though your arm moves forward into an ideal throwing position, your tip is still laid back. So, you are not *creeping* the rod's tip forward in a way that detracts from your next cast.

Drift after the forward cast. Although you usually hear about drifting on your back cast, some skilled casters drift after the forward cast as well. When stopping a forward false cast, you can drift your rod and hand lower to create additional space in which to lift the rod during the next back cast. On the final forward cast, however, your casting arm is drifted more upward after the stop. This final follow-through movement can set the rod angle for more efficient line shoot through the rod's guides, reduce a stiff rod's shock to your casting arm, and help dampen the final downward tip movements of the fly rod (figure 8-3).

How do you teach adding drift to your cast? Jim Green taught a little drift while teaching a basic cast. He stopped the back cast at one o'clock, then softened the wrist enough to allow the rod to *drift* back a little farther. Softening the wrist in this way is the beginning of a drift that adds rod angle.

I believe that most instructors delay teaching drift until students have learned a basic cast. Joan Wulff has taught stopping the back cast, then raising the casting arm just enough to move the hand up and back a few inches. In raising and straightening the elbow a bit, she has added slight movements at both the elbow and shoulder joints. Lefty's style of drift also extends the arm at the shoulder and elbow, but in a more horizontal, sidearm plane.

I wait to teach drift until I have added most other movements to a distance cast. I do this once again by practicing hand movements first, then adding an unstrung fly rod, and finally adding the fly line to the rod.

Figure 8-3. Drift in the final forward cast (1) starts where the rod starts decelerating and (2) ends at the final reach position.

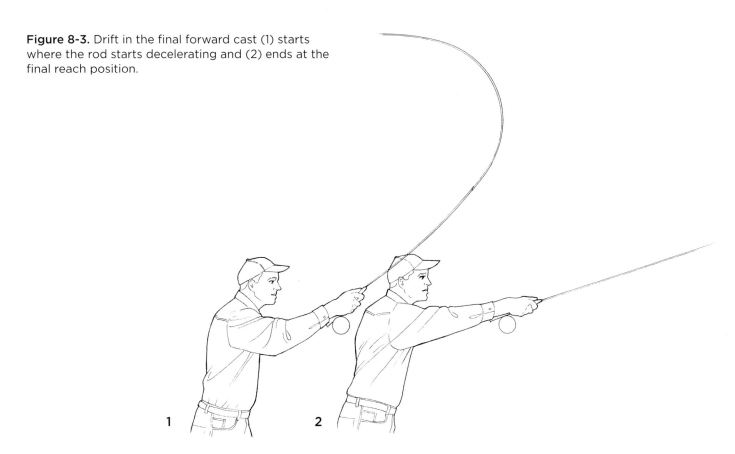

PRACTICE #14: DRIFT HAND PANTOMIME

Pantomiming your drift movements without the fly rod can help your learning. If you use an elbow-forward casting style, make your back-cast movement by lifting your hand back and up to stop at ear level with your forearm vertical. Then add your drift movement by raising your arm a little more from the shoulder. Finish with a forward casting motion. You might call these steps *lift, drift, cast* (figure 8-4). If you use a low-elbow style, make your usual stop, then drift your hand back and up a little farther before making your cast forward (figure 8-5).

Repeat these movements until the two backward stops are less distinct. Once you begin to smooth them out, try them with an unstrung fly rod as well.

PRACTICE #15: ADDING THE FLY LINE TO YOUR DRIFT PRACTICE

Now string up your rod and strip out as much line as

Figure 8-4. Pantomiming back-cast drift with (1) lift, (2) drift, and (3) cast hand positions.

Figure 8-5. Pantomiming back-cast drift with low-elbow style with (1) lift, (2) drift, and (3) cast hand positions.

you can comfortably handle with only your rod hand, making casts that land the fly about forty to forty-five feet from where you stand. As you do this, make a short back cast, if anything a little shorter than usual. You do this to leave additional room for a second backward movement after the stop. Then make that second movement, your drift movement, by lifting your hand up and back a few more inches as you did without a fly line. As soon as you complete that movement, make your forward cast. It may take a few false casts to remember to add a second backward movement to your initial stop. Even then, I would expect you to make a jerky stop and a second backward movement with another distinct stop. With practice, however, your movements become smoother and your stops become less obvious.

PRACTICE #16: ADDING DRIFT TO PREVIOUS DISTANCE DRILLS

When your drift movements are no longer jerky, turn back to Practice #11 where you started adding stroke length to a distance cast. Open up your stance and rock your body back and forth as you did before. But this time, don't reach your hand farther back. Instead, make a short, controlled back cast, and use drift to move that hand farther back. You can extend your hand forward as you did before on your final forward cast. This shorter initial back cast should give you tighter back-cast loops than you previously had when doing this practice.

Then, turn to Practice #12, in which you lowered your back cast and raised your forward cast. Now do this by making your short back-cast stop and then letting your rod tip drift low enough to help set up an upward-angled tip path for the forward cast. You are using drift to increase rod angle and tip travel for the next forward cast as well as tilting your casting plane.

So, drift is a follow-through movement to reposition the rod after a casting stroke. It can add stroke length, rod angle and speed, maintain tension to the fly line, change the rod's tilt, allow you to reposition the casting arm, and provide a cushion against the shock of stopping a stiff rod. Essentially, it is a transition movement that provides a way to link a short, controlled back-cast movement with the longer, wider movement needed to drive a long forward cast.

CHAPTER 9

ADDING THE DOUBLE HAUL

The double haul is important to your distance casting. Hauling, or pulling on the fly line, can add speed to that line, which enables you to carry more of it through the air. This speed also helps to control the fly line, takes pressure off the work of the rod hand, and helps drive the line into a wind. In effect, it allows you to cast farther with less effort. A double haul is two pulls with your line hand, the first coming during the back cast, the second, during the forward cast. The speed comes from both pulling line through the rod, which speeds up the line beyond the tip, and from increasing the rod's bend and subsequent spring effect.

Although important to distance fly fishing, the double haul is seldom easy to learn. You may find the movements difficult to coordinate or the conflicting advice on technique confusing. Experts variously recommend hauls that are long, short, fast, or slow. They may recommend starting your hauling movement as you start moving the rod or later in the cast. Making sense out of these different recommendations should help you to simplify this important dimension of casting.

The final haul of the forward cast. In studying the double haul, I was most interested in the last haul that releases line into a long forward cast. In our distance casting study, the casters with the most effective hauls typically moved the hauling hand the fastest after the rod's butt had been rotated forward of vertical, and released

the line at the end of the haul as the rod tip deflected downward after the cast. These casters were using a weight-forward floating fly line.

When I looked at film of some of these same casters double hauling with a shooting-taper line, I noticed that they made longer, earlier hauls and released line from the hauling hand earlier in the rod's unloading as well. So the difference between hauling monofilament or fly line through the rod is enough to account for some of the different recommendations as to speed, length, and timing of hauls. You need to know the type of line being cast.

I believe the fly rod you use also affects the speed and timing of your hauling. A fast hauling movement matches up naturally with a rod that loads and unloads quickly, such as a tip-flex rod, whereas a slower moving haul corresponds well with a rod that loads and unloads slowly, such as a full-flex rod.

Even the purpose of my cast affects how I haul. I most often use a quick, short haul to tighten up my casting loops, a longer slower haul to regain feel when smoothing out my timing, and a long quick haul to impart high energy to the fly line for my longest casts. So differences in equipment and casting purpose have influenced me to carefully avoid making simple recommendations of only one type of haul.

I think it is important to understand the relationship between the line hand's pull and the fly rod's movements. Whatever time your rod hand takes to initially start bending the rod and moving the fly line, your line hand should take to haul slowly enough to help control that bend to guide the tip along a straight path. Whatever time your rod hand takes to accelerate the tip through the rod's final rotation, stop, and straightening, your line hand should take to haul fast. We sometimes teach coordinating the speed of the hauling hand to the speed of the rod hand. However, what moves fast together is the rod's tip and the hauling hand. This difference becomes most apparent when

you watch footage of a caster's rod hand coming to a stop, and notice that the *hauling hand* and *rod tip* are still moving fast.

Teaching the double haul. If the rod hand and hauling hand do not always move fast at the same time, why do we teach as if they do? I know of two reasons. First, moving both hands fast at the same time can work well with shooting-taper lines. Second, teaching both hands to move together simplifies learning to coordinate the movements of both hands. When both hands do different things at the same time, as when hauling, it is easier for most learners to start moving those hands together. This is true in teaching a tennis serve as well, where it often helps to say "down together, up together," to guide the coordinated timing of one hand that is taking the racquet back with one that is tossing the ball. So, in teaching the double haul, I first teach the generalized hauling movement pattern with both hands starting and moving together, and, at some later point, adjust that coordination to the more precise, later timing demands of a weight-forward fly line.

PRACTICE #17: MEL KRIEGER'S PANTOMIME

Many casting instructors have adopted Mel Krieger's method for introducing the double haul by pantomiming the hand movements without a rod or fly line. That technique has worked so well for me that I now use pantomime practices for other simpler casting movements as well.

In this practice, you make a back-cast motion with your dominant hand holding an imaginary fly rod, while your other hand pulls down on an imaginary fly line and immediately moves it back up toward the rod hand. Then, as your rod hand makes an imaginary forward cast, the line hand again pulls down and back up. The upward movement resets your line hand to make the next haul.

Mel speaks of these line-hand movements as *downup*—two movements in one word, to emphasize the lack of any stop after the downward part. So you say "downup" during your back-cast hand movements (figure 9-1) and say "downup" again during your forward-cast hand movements (figure 9-2).

Some people teach a single haul first. I intentionally do not, because it can interfere with, rather than benefit, the learning of a double haul. Learning to complete the *up* part of the *downup* movement (without hesitation) is critical to your success in learning the double haul and needs to be emphasized from the outset of your practice. Many people learn the single haul first by pulling down on their haul but leaving that hand down. This is exactly what you do *not* want to do when learning a double haul. In fact, it is a habit that is not easy to break. So, I prefer to teach the double haul first. It is then an easy matter to haul on only the back cast or only the forward cast if you wish.

Figure 9-1. Pantomiming line hand's "downup" path during the back cast.

Figure 9-2. Line hand's "downup" path during the forward cast.

PRACTICE #18: ADDING THE ROD BUTT AND RUBBER BAND

Some people have trouble visualizing what their pantomiming hand movements represent: it all seems too abstract. So as a follow-up step, I now have students continue these downup movements while holding the butt half of a fly rod in the rod hand and one end of a long rubber band in the line hand. The other end of that three-foot-long rubber band is knotted to the stripping guide of the rod butt. You move the rod butt to effectively communicate a fly rod's backward and forward movements, and haul on the rubber band, which gives you an exaggerated feel of the line's tension and reminds you to complete the *up* part of the *downup*. So you never stop the rubber band in a stretched or down position. I make these rubber bands by cutting and knotting together three of the largest rubber bands I can buy at a stationery store (size 117B), and each is a foot long when cut. This practice also allows you to watch your hands to avoid the common error of starting the haul before the rod's movement. If you haul early in the movement, you are applying excessive force early, which depresses the rod tip to throw a tailing loop into the line. If anything, start the rod butt moving, then make your haul.

When you feel the coordination of these movements, try them with your rod and fly line. I like Mel's idea of starting with a short, easy-to-manage, twenty-five-foot shooting head (i.e., shooting-taper line), over-lined for the rod. Having this entire fly line beyond the rod tip intensifies the feel of the line's responsiveness to your pulling and recovering movements.

PRACTICE #19: DOUBLE HAULING WITH A PART METHOD

For some people, the timing of the hauls comes only after breaking the cast into two parts, practicing one haul at a time. To do this, start with the line on the grass in front of you, with the shooting head and about five feet of

running line beyond the rod tip. The amount of running line beyond the tip is called *overhang*. Start by making your back cast, executing your downup haul as you do, and letting the line fall to the grass behind you. Do not let go of the line during this practice. Take a moment to check that your line hand has completed the up movement toward your rod. Then take a few steps forward if needed to straighten the line on the grass and make your forward cast with a second downup haul. This should return the line to the grass in front of you.

Continue your "downup" movements with a long rubber band and rod butt. Start your forward cast (1) with hands together, then (2) make your haul during the last part of the movement, and as soon as you feel the rubber band stretching, (3) complete the "up" movement back toward the rod.

When you have repeated these movements enough to feel confident, combine the two hauls with the line moving back and forth in the air. False casting while hauling increases your feel of the line and the timing that works. Sometimes I stand behind a student and move both of his or her arms to communicate the feel of the two hands working together. I call that my puppet practice. If your student is much larger than you are, this practice is difficult to do. Yet you could still help by standing on the line-hand side of the student and hauling with your hand holding the student's line hand as he or she moves the fly rod back and forth.

PRACTICE #20: SHOOTING LINE ON THE FINAL HAUL

Next you need to learn how to shoot line on your final haul. Practice this release without false casting. In other words, lift your line off the grass in front with your back cast, making your first downup haul. Then, with the line straightening in the air behind you, make your forward cast. As you do, pull the line down and back, releasing it when your line hand is farthest back and your rod and arm extended forward. On this last, line-releasing haul, there is no up movement.

Emphasize the feel of the last haul by pulling line back behind your body before releasing.

PRACTICE #21: HAULING WITH A WEIGHT-FORWARD LINE

When double hauling with a weight-forward line, you are pulling a thick fly line, rather than a thin running line, through the rod guides. Adjusting to this added resistance may require shortening your hauls and delaying the timing. With forty to fifty feet of fly line on the grass, use the *part method* again—this time with a sidearm cast. Start moving both hands back together to the side and, about halfway through your sidearm back cast, make a short haul. The line moving on the grass should become airborne with your haul and fall to the

Sidearm hauling practice allows you to watch (1) the cast starting to move the line, (2) the hands staying together through the first half of the movement, and (3) the line lifting off the grass with your haul. Let the line fall to the grass and do the same with your forward cast.

1

2

3

grass again behind your rod. Take a few steps forward to straighten the line on the grass. Then start forward with both hands together, and halfway through your sidearm forward cast, make your second haul. Continue back and forth, eventually keeping the line in the air, as you combine the hauls. If slack forms between your hauling hand and the stripping guide, shorten your hauls even more. Practicing sidearm gives you the opportunity to watch your rod movements in relation to your hauling movements.

Even if you have previously learned the double haul, this is a good practice sequence to tune up your timing prior to a fishing trip. More people than ever are scheduling trips for species that demand distance fly casting. You have already learned ways to gain casting distance by increasing your stroke length, angular rotation, up/down tilt, and drift. Adding the double haul allows you to experience what additional speed brings as well. If you can put these pieces together, you are likely to find yourself casting farther than ever before.

Part III

BETTER PROBLEM SOLVING

CHAPTER 10

LEARNING YOUR FLY ROD— ONE MOVEMENT AT A TIME

The more I have tested and analyzed fly rods and felt subtle differences between them, the more I have come to appreciate how special a good fly rod is. This was put into perspective for me when our study on distance casting was presented at the International Symposium on Biomechanics in Sports in 1991. Scientists who had no interest in fishing were fascinated by the prolonged control that a fly cast provides over the movement of a flexible lever. Apparently they had not found this in any other sports equipment—fishing or otherwise.

Controlling that flexible fly rod can be frustrating, however: slight differences in your hand's movements are transmitted up through the rod to throw a fly line off its intended course. Yet, for those who are persistent, this control can become a source of increasing pleasure. Such control is what impresses me most about the great casters—the control to be able to consistently throw beautiful casting loops, regardless of changes in casting conditions or equipment.

Your own control over the fly rod should already be getting better from what you have been practicing, particularly in alternating between the compact movements of a short cast and the more extended movements of a distance cast. In this chapter I want you to gain even more control over your fly rod by varying one movement at a time and observing what happens to the fly line as you do.

In the casting practices in this chapter, the control between what your hand does and what the fly line does will be helped by several things. One is casting with a firm-enough wrist movement (regardless of casting style) to eliminate any looseness between your hand and the fly rod. Another is eliminating any line-hand errors or hauling weaknesses by casting with your rod hand only. A third is keeping all rod movements as much the same as possible, except the one you are intentionally changing. If, for example, you are varying the angle the rod rotates through, you need to minimize any changes in stroke length, speed, or up/down tilt.

For each of these practices, strip out enough line to make casts that land the fly about forty feet from where you stand. This distance should be long enough to clearly see differences in your fly line, yet short enough to cast comfortably with only your rod hand. The leader you have been using should work well. The 2X tippet is strong enough to handle the abuse of repeated casts, and the 7½-foot length is short enough to continue whatever movement you transmit to the fly line. If, for example, you cast a hard curve into your fly line, that curve is much more likely to be transmitted throughout the length of a 7½-foot leader than a 12-foot leader. So, the construction of your leader has a pronounced effect on how the fly is presented. Yet here you keep the leader dimensions constant to be able learn the fly rod's role in changing that presentation.

For this practice, use a fly rod that is light enough to be easy to cast—perhaps your favorite trout rod. The taper of that rod should not make much difference. I have recently done these practices with two Orvis rods that are extremely different in taper design and material—an early-generation graphite, full-flex, 4-weight Superfine 711 (i.e., seven feet eleven inches), and a new tip-flex, nine-foot, 5-weight Zero G rod. The fly line responds in the same general ways to my movements with either rod.

People who are accustomed to casting mid-flex or tip-flex rods sometimes have trouble controlling line with a slower full-flex rod. The experts in our study, when forced to switch from tip-flex to full-flex rods, adjusted by widening the angle of rotation, lengthening the casting stroke, and/or slowing their movements. In different ways, each of these adjustments keeps the fly line under the influence of the rod tip longer—either a longer distance or a longer time.

During the following practices, you will learn to vary the movement of the fly rod in nine different ways. You are already familiar with the first four—angular rotation, stroke length, and up/down tilt, speed. You will also practice varying the timing of applying force to the forward cast and experiment with pushing or pulling the tip forward. In each of those six movements, your rod is held upright and its tip should follow a straight forward and backward path (i.e., technically called the *sagittal plane of movement*). The final three movements are departures from this overhead cast—offsetting the rod tip before, during, and after the forward cast.

PRACTICE #22: CHANGING ONLY ANGULAR ROTATION

As you recall, angular rotation changes when you widen or narrow the angle the rod rotates through. Typically you do this by using more wrist and/or elbow motion to widen the angle and less of that motion to narrow it. Start this practice by false casting these same forty-foot casts to control your casting loops, then add wrist and/or elbow movement to gradually let the rod angle widen, making your back casts stop farther back and your forward casts stop farther forward. After widening the angle as much as seems practical, start narrowing it again. When you have narrowed the angle as much as you can, gradually widen again. Alternate between widening and narrowing and observe. How has this movement affected your fly line?

Whenever I widen my rod angle in this practice, my casting loops get wider and change shape by *opening up*. Whenever I narrow the rod angle, my casting loops usually become narrow and more parallel in shape, eventually closing enough to *tail* or at least *tick* my rod tip (figure 10-1). How does that happen?

When you widen the rod's angle without changing the force or speed of your cast, your rod's tip starts following a convex or *windshield-wiper* path. This is because the rod tip is being dropped lower on both stops. As the angle narrows, this tip path flattens out again. With an extremely narrow angle, too little distance remains for the rod tip to smoothly pull that amount of fly line along a straight path. The extra force needed to complete the cast causes the rod to bend more, which deflects the tip downward into a concave or *saucer-shaped* path. This results in a tailing loop in the line that follows. So changing only the rod angle moves the rod tip up or down off of its straight path and is most likely to change the *shape* of your casting loops—widening the angle opens the shape, narrowing closes it. Adjusting this angle of rotation gains importance whenever your loop shape needs correction.

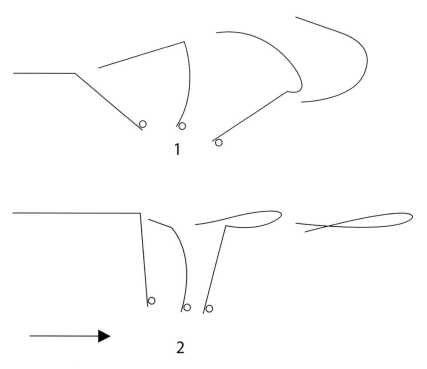

Figure 10-1. Wide angular rotation (1) invites a convex (windshield-wiper) tip path and open loop shape, whereas narrow angular rotation (2) invites a concave (saucer) tip path and tailing loop shape.

PRACTICE #23: CHANGING ONLY STROKE LENGTH

You vary stroke length, or rod butt travel, by changing the distance your casting hand moves the rod butt toward your casting direction. So as you continue false casting forty-foot casts, gradually start lengthening your back and forward hand movements—more forward on the forward cast and back on the back cast. You try to keep all other rod movements, including the rod angle, the same. After reaching your longest hand movements, gradually shorten them until they are as short as possible. Alternate between lengthening and shortening your hand movement. What happens to your fly line as a result of changing only the stroke length?

At this forty-foot distance, I found it awkward to cast with extremely long hand movements—too much wasted motion. Yet, as you might expect, these longer strokes felt more natural when casting the shorter, full-flex rod. When shortening the stroke length to the extreme, the loops occasionally started to tail, most noticeably with the full-flex rod. Yet, whether lengthening or shortening the stroke, most of the casting loops were well shaped and similar in size.

In this practice, you have been casting at one distance only: forty feet. However, the benefits of changing stroke length are most evident when you need to vary the distance of your casts. Such changes in stroke length allow you to vary the distance your rod tip travels to accommodate different combinations of speed, rod bend, and rod angle.

Short stroke.

Long stroke.

PRACTICE #24: CHANGING ONLY UP/DOWN TILT

You raise or lower the direction of your forward cast (i.e., target line) by tilting your cast backward or forward. You do this by changing where your rod stops. As you start false casting in this practice, gradually lower your forward target line by tilting your cast forward until your fly line almost ticks the ground in front. Do not widen the angle, just tilt the same angle forward—stopping higher in back and lower in front (figure 10-2). Then gradually tilt that cast backward to raise your forward target line until your fly line straightens well above horizontal. As you raise the forward cast, lower your stop in back—to keep the fly line moving along a straight path from the back cast through the forward cast.

Alternating between short casting strokes and longer casting strokes teaches movement variation that becomes important when you change casting distance.

What changes did you notice in these casts? If you kept the rod angle the same as you tilted the casts backward or forward, and kept the line in back straightening behind the line in front, your casting loops should all have been similar: well shaped. So changing the tilt in this way should not produce an error, just good loops thrown higher or lower (figure 10-3). Your ability to vary this movement can be important both in changing how the fly line moves through the air and how it falls to the water.

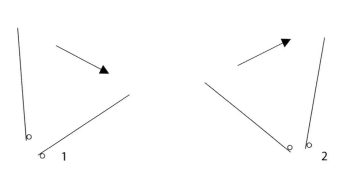

Figure 10-2. Up/down tilt: To aim your forward cast lower, (1) tilt your cast forward. To aim it higher, (2) tilt your cast back.

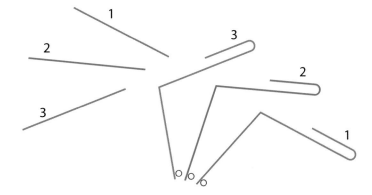

Figure 10-3. Changing up/down tilt teaches you to cast effectively into lower or higher angles, which affects how your line and fly move through the air and fall to the water to vary your presentation.

PRACTICE #25: CHANGING SPEED

Being able to vary how much you bend your rod allows you to keep the rod tip moving along a straight path, whether casting long or short. When casting at one particular distance, you change bend by changing the amount of force you apply to the rod, including any acceleration. In experimenting with changing the rod's bend, I found I was not able to separate the strength I applied from the speed I added. Whenever I added strength, my hand also wanted to move faster. I concluded that the simplest way for someone to practice changing and controlling rod bend is to change the speed your rod hand moves. As you do, the force and rod bend also change. (When you add the line hand, your haul can increase speed further.)

Using only your rod hand false casting at forty feet, gradually speed up your movements until moving your rod back and forth rapidly. Then start slowing down until you are barely able to keep your line moving over the rod's tip. Alternate between fast and slow movements. What happens to your fly line as you make these changes?

As I practiced this, I noticed two distinct changes in my casts. The faster my hand moved the rod butt, the faster the line moved. The casting loops also became somewhat narrower. As my movements slowed, the loops widened and the line moved slower. Yet, for the most part, the loops remained well shaped. On extremely slow casting movements, the loop shape sometimes opened up, and on the fastest movements, it sometimes started to tail. When attempting to move the full-flex rod rapidly, the fly line sometimes hit the rod tip, which needed more time to unload and straighten. A slow-recovering rod just isn't designed to be moved fast.

Some people appear to make all their casts at the same speed—usually fast enough to take advantage of the distance potential that speed brings. However, decreasing speed can help present a fly delicately as well as heighten your feel of the rod's movement. So changing the speed of your movement provides a way to adjust both the speed of the moving fly line and the size of your casting loop.

PRACTICE #26: CHANGING THE TIMING OF FORCE APPLICATION

When you think of timing in an overhead cast, it is usually the timing between the back cast and forward cast. In this practice, however, you vary the timing of applying sudden force to your forward cast—early or late in the movement. I have previously emphasized a smooth casting movement, but you can also learn things about control

Increasing hand speed (1) adds rod bend and line speed and reduces loop size in comparison to a slower movement (2).

1

2

by applying sudden force. Emphasizing force late in the movement is one of the most difficult things about a fly cast to teach. Overdoing that force can help teach the precise timing of a hard stop. One way to learn this timing is to contrast it to an early application of force—just as you start your forward cast. Practicing this contrast and feeling the difference can help you develop a more precise feel.

In this practice, start your false casts by applying abrupt force as you stop your forward cast. In the casting style I teach, I first lower my elbow a little, then apply the force to stop—by pressing the thumb. After a few of these casts, try applying sudden force as you start your forward cast. Alternate between the two. What happened to your fly line during these changes?

When I practice this, applying force early usually causes my loops to tail. Applying force as I stop usually results in well-shaped loops. This practice emphasizes the difference between starting forward smoothly and shocking the rod, and it can also give you the feel of applying excessive force as you stop. *Shocking* the rod by applying sudden force as you start the cast depresses your rod tip, causing the line coming behind to tail. Applying excessive force as you stop causes the rod tip to deflect sharply downward. This can drive the path of the fly line downward in a short cast or put waves in the line beyond the tip in a long cast, sometimes causing the end of the fly line to bounce back toward you. Certain specialty casts depend on such overpowering for their effectiveness.

PRACTICE #27: PULLING OR PUSHING THE FLY ROD

For some years I was confused by casting instructors who urged thrusting, stabbing, or breaking the balloon to make the forward cast. These instructors seemed to be recommending a pushing motion forward, as in thrusting a sword with the point forward.

This is different from pulling the tip around. When pulling the rod forward, its tip lags behind, like a ball-throwing hand, and is the last part of the rod to come forward. This movement illustrates the throwing mechanics of the kinetic whip referred to earlier, in which you use big muscles of the body and shoulder to start bending the butt of the rod, then transfer energy progressively to the weaker, but faster, muscles of the arm and wrist to provide the final speed to bring the tip around.

In a pulling movement, the pressure to bend the rod starts down in the butt and progresses up the rod to roll off the tip. With a pushing motion, however, the rod is rotated forward before the primary force is applied and the thrusting movement creates bend higher in the tip.

One blustery Alaska day a few years ago, the cold had robbed me of the hand strength needed to force bend into the butt of a stiff 10-weight rod. The only way I could load that rod was to rotate it forward early and push bend into the more yielding tip. Suddenly, I saw an advantage of being able to bring the rod forward in a different way.

To practice these contrasting movements, start with a series of false casts in which you smoothly pull the tip around, pressing your thumb to stop the cast. Then make another series in which you start by rotating the rod enough to be able to push or thrust the tip forward toward the direction of your cast. Alternate these two movements every few casts trying to keep the rod angle and stroke length the same. What did you notice?

At forty feet, I can get similar casting loops with either of these movements as long as I keep the tip moving smoothly. What I like most about practicing pushing the tip forward is how good it feels to go back to smoothly pulling the tip around. Although varying this rod movement may not change the path of your fly line, it should increase your awareness of your own tendency to either push or pull the fly rod forward. This experimentation could result in a casting movement that works better for you than what you have been doing. Although most instructors teach pulling the tip around, the stiff butt sections of many of today's larger saltwater rods invite slightly built fly fishers to add a little push to force bend into the tip.

DEPARTURES FROM THE OVERHEAD CAST

When fishing, you don't always want the fly line to land straight in front of you on the water. Most specialty casts move the rod tip away from a vertical, straight back and forward path. You can do this by offsetting your rod tip either before, during, or after the forward cast. In the next three practices, you will work on different techniques for offsetting the tip to one side or the other. To do this *before* the cast, you tilt or cant the rod off to one side. Your rod tip is still moving straight back and forward, but shifts from an upright to an increasingly horizontal plane. To offset the rod tip *during* the cast, you return to your overhead movement but start angling your rod tip's movement off to one side as soon as you start your for-

ward cast. To move the tip off to one side *after* the cast, you make an overhead cast, then move the tip to one side after stopping the rod yet before the fly line lands.

To me, the purest form of an overhead cast is keeping the fly rod upright and moving the fly line back and forward directly above its tip. Yet many anglers cast normally with the rod canted down a little to the side. In effect, these casters are already using the first of these techniques for offsetting the tip.

PRACTICE #28: TILTING THE ROD TO THE SIDE

In this practice, start with a few false casts overhead, then gradually tilt your rod downward on your casting side, continuing until you are casting sidearm. The way I do this is to keep changing the angle of my forearm to remain aligned with the fly rod. As the rod moves from vertical toward horizontal, so does my forearm. When you are finally casting sidearm, gradually raise your rod again and continue up to and beyond vertical to tilt your rod down on your non-casting side. To keep your forearm aligned with your rod on that side, let your casting elbow move out and up from your casting side. Tilting your upper body down to that side also helps achieve a sidearm cast on that side of your body. What does your line flow look like during these casts?

In this practice, you should be able to cast well-shaped loops at all of these angles. The line moves lower and off to the side as you lower the rod tip. Your loops also should unroll more from the side—in an increasingly horizontal plane. Tilting the rod to a side helps to avoid obstructions or wind on your casting side, as well as branches that overhang your fish's lie.

PRACTICE #29: CHANGING TIP DIREC- TION DURING THE FORWARD CAST

Whenever your rod tip moves away from a straight forward-backward path, your fly line is pulled off that path

as well. You can see this in your casting loop whenever your wrist accidentally turns slightly or your hand moves off to one side during your forward cast. Such slight movement is enough to move your rod tip off to the side and tilt your casting loop.

As you continue to false cast at forty feet, start angling your casting hand off to the right on the forward cast. Start to the side with your first forward movement. As you do so, your rod tip is "painting" a straight line above you that also veers off to the right. On your back cast, return your hand and rod to a vertical alignment for the next forward cast. Then angle the next forward cast off to the left. Alternate between angling to the right and left on successive casts, returning the rod to an upright position with each back cast. How does your fly line look different than usual?

When I angle my forward movement to the right in this way, the rod tip pulls the lower part of my casting loop and the fly line below that loop off to the right.

Moving the rod tip to the left during the cast moves the bottom part of the loop and the lower part of the line off to the left. Learning to control the rod in this way begins to open up options for laying your fly line on the water

Raising the casting arm and tilting the body to the side can help to lower the rod toward horizontal on your non-casting side.

in various angles or curves. The rod movement taught here is the one I use to reach the line off to one side in what is generally known as a reach cast.

PRACTICE #30: OFFSETTING THE TIP AFTER THE STOP

When you stop a typical forward cast, there is still time to move the rod tip in some direction before the line drops to the water. Rod adjustments during this time are generally referred to as *aerial mends*. Although not generally considered to be part of the cast, these movements are often critical to your fishing presentation.

In this practice, make a typical overhead false cast. As you stop the forward cast, immediately move your hand and rod off to the right. Then, while your line is still in the air, use your back cast to realign your hand and rod upright again. As you stop the next forward cast, move your hand over to the left. Continue to alternate directions on successive casts. This practice is similar to the previous

1

2

Rod tip (1) offset to the left early enough in the cast to pull the loop to the side as well as the line below and (2) offset to the right after the vertical loop has been formed (aerial mend).

one, except that your movement of the rod tip over to the side occurs later—after, rather than throughout, the forward movement (figure 10-4). What difference do you notice in the fly line between these two practices?

In watching my casts, I noticed that these loops unrolled more vertically, although the later tip movement did pull the lower leg of fly line off to the side as before. Aerial mends can be made in several directions and combinations, which further open up possibilities for fishing. A tip-flexing rod recovers so quickly that you can achieve the same straight reach-cast layout of line on the water as you did when off-setting the tip during the cast.

PRACTICE #31: COMBINING THESE PRACTICES INTO A SINGLE WARM-UP

My favorite way to work on control of my fly rod's movements is to combine these nine practices into a single warm-up. As I start false casting, I first change the speed of my hand movement, then the length of the hand

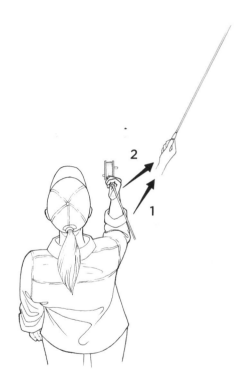

Figure 10-4. Moving the rod tip to one side (1) during the forward cast or (2) after the stop (aerial mend).

stroke, then the angle the rod moves through, then the up/down tilt. Then I hit extra force early and late, push and pull the tip through, tilt the cast to one side and the other, move the tip over during the forward cast and then after the stop. If I take three or four false casts with each movement, I have practiced controlling a variety of rod adjustments, and done so in only a couple of minutes. You may initially need to take a three-by-five card with you to your casting area with key words written down to guide your sequence. This one practice allows you to vary a fly rod's movements in more ways than most fly fishers know how to do. You are also warming up your cast by making many of the casting adjustments you will use in one form or another to solve problems when fishing.

If that warm-up seems too complicated, start simply by combining only the four most basic movements—speed, stroke length, angle of rotation, and up/down tilt. When doing this, you might think of the word *SLAT* as a reminder to vary the *Speed, Length, Angle,* and *Tilt* of your cast.

CHAPTER 11

COMBINING YOUR FLY ROD'S MOVEMENTS

Learning to control your fly rod by varying one move-ment at a time may have been a new type of practice for you. What you have probably been doing instead is try-ing to eliminate all variation to become more consistent from one cast to the next. Control comes through both strategies. Initially, you achieve control by trying to do everything the same. But, at some point, control comes by deviating from that "grooved" movement to be able to adapt to different rods, fly lines, and fishing conditions. The great casters adjust to differences without seeming to do anything different. Yet, frame-by-frame analysis of their casts reveals the rod changes they are making. This ability to adapt to differences clearly differentiated the best distance casters in our studies from the advanced anglers who were less successful.

In this chapter, you continue learning to vary your movements—but now by varying two movements in combination. You are moving further into the world of the specialty cast.

COMBINING FAMILIAR MOVEMENTS

Speed and angle of rotation. Combining two rod movements can accomplish different things, one of which is to reinforce and exaggerate something you achieved with a single rod movement. For example, if you combine widening the rod angle, which opens up the casting loop, with slowing your movement, which widens and slows the loop, you should be able to move the fly line forward with a loop so open and wide that it appears not to be

a loop at all. In fact, Mel Krieger has long taught and referred to this extremely wide, open movement of line as a *non-loop* (figure 11-1). As instructors, we use this combination to demonstrate the opposite error of a tailing loop. To return from that wide non-loop to a parallel loop, you narrow the angle and move faster.

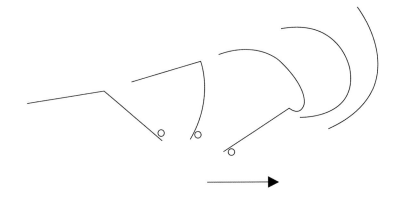

Figure 11-1. Combining wide angular rotation with slow movement to illustrate a "non-loop."

You can combine these same two rod movements in a different way to achieve a different outcome. If you speed your movements up as you widen the rod angle, rather than slow down, you can maintain the same parallel loop shape as you move from short to long casts. If you start short with a narrow rod angle and slow speed, you can cast with small, well-shaped loops. As you start casting farther, you can add speed to your movement and widen the rod angle to continue getting good loops. On even longer casts, you can move the rod so fast and widen the angle so far that you are bending the entire rod—yet still throw small loops. Widening the angle lowers the rod tip at both the beginning and end of a cast, and adding speed lowers that tip during the cast. So varying these two movements together helps you maintain a straight rod-tip path whether casting a short line with little speed or a long line with more speed. Understanding this relationship has allowed casting instructors to understand why the teaching concept *wide angle, wide loops* is sometimes not true.

Narrow angle of rotation and early force application. Combining a narrow angle of rotation with an early force application offers another example of two movements that reinforce each other to magnify what you do to the fly line. In chapter 10, you found that narrowing the angle to its extreme in a forty-foot cast invited a tailing loop. Hitting the cast with sudden force at the start of the forward cast also produced a tailing loop. When you combine the two, you can achieve an even more pronounced tailing loop. What has surprised me most about having to certify potential casting instructors is that some of these experienced casters failed their test because they were unable to demonstrate a tailing loop. They had "grooved" their parallel loops well, but could not vary from that movement pattern. Sometimes an instructor needs to be able to demonstrate casting errors to students. Varying your movements—even practicing errors—increases your control over your fly rod and line.

Up/down tilt and late force application. If you stop your forward cast with excessive force, you deflect the rod's tip downward at the end of the cast (after the rod has straightened), which directs the path of the line and leader downward past horizontal. On a short cast, this downward path allows your fly to contact the water first. If you also adjust the angle of your stops to raise your forward cast, you have created a high pivot point and additional distance for your leader to swing around even more downward toward vertical. Any weight on or near the fly you are fishing adds to this effect. This combination is widely known as a *tuck cast,* which is useful whenever you need to have your leader cut through the surface currents to help sink your fly quickly. I also use this combination when fishing a dry fly and nymph together in pocket water only a rod's length upstream. In this short tuck cast, I want the downward swing of the leader completed so the dry fly swings around and stops just above the water's surface. Then I gently lower that dry fly the last few inches to start the drift. This gentle drop keeps my fly floating much more consistently in mixed currents than when letting it hit the water on the cast.

Side tilt and late force application. The same principle is commonly used in a horizontal plane. Growing up fishing in small creeks, my first specialty cast was a sidearm overpowered cast to get my fly back under overhanging foliage. As a boy, I did not know I was teaching myself to make a positive curve cast. Changing the casting plane to sidearm lowers the fly line and sets up a horizontally formed loop that, when overpowered at the stop, moves the rod's tip, leader, and fly around farther than usual. The challenge is to get the fly back far enough to catch the fish before the bush catches the fly.

Historically, a positive curve cast has to do with *positive* or excessive force applied as the cast is stopped. When a right-handed caster tilts the rod down to the right side, the overpowered, or positive, energy sends the curve around to the left. When that same caster tilts the rod over to the left side of the body to make a horizontal cast to the right, the overpowered, positive curve bends to the right. A negative curve is an underpowered cast, whether made from the left or right side.

COMBINING MOVEMENTS TO MAKE A STRAIGHT ANGLE CHANGE IN YOUR FLY LINE

Moving the rod tip over and back. If, as you make a forward cast, you move the rod tip off to one side and quickly back again after stopping the cast, your line falls to the water angled to one side and back. The sooner your hand moves over and back in your casting movement, the farther from you that angle appears on the water. You can learn this technique by starting a reach cast, then almost immediately returning the rod tip straight forward again. At first, the angle on the water is likely to fall close to your rod tip. But as you practice starting and

completing this movement earlier in your cast, that angle should appear ever closer to your leader.

If you alternate several of these side-to-side movements, the fly line falls to the water in a series of zig-zags. Tilting back to raise your forward cast provides additional air time for more zig-zags to form. How fast and far you move your hand or wiggle your wrist from side to side determines the number and width of the zig-zag angles that fall to the water. This combination of movements has been called names such as wiggle cast, S-cast, and serpentine cast and is probably best used to fish a dry fly directly downstream on even-flowing water.

COMBINING MOVEMENTS TO FORM A CURVE IN THE FLY LINE

If you move your rod tip over and back with a curving hand motion, the angles soften to form curves on the water. One common way to do this is to make an aerial mend in the form of a letter C from high to low (figure

11-2). To make a curve to the right and back to the left, you draw a backward C with your hand and rod tip.

I even use a slight curving movement on most of my back casts. I start my back cast by tilting the rod slightly to the side to move my line barely outside of and above the rod tip. I continue that curving movement by returning my hand and rod to vertical to complete the back cast. The fly line should straighten almost directly behind my forward cast. If, instead, I were to continue angling the back cast movement off to the side, the fly line would continue angling off to the side as well. On a long back cast, this angled line would send the fly well off to that side, requiring it to be swung around inefficiently behind the rod tip before coming forward (figure 11-3).

Continuing the curving path to form an oval. If, after making that slight curving back-cast movement, you continue by curving to the opposite side during your

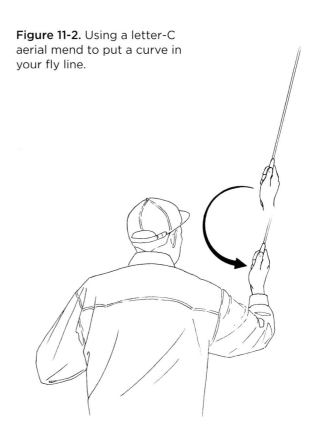

Figure 11-2. Using a letter-C aerial mend to put a curve in your fly line.

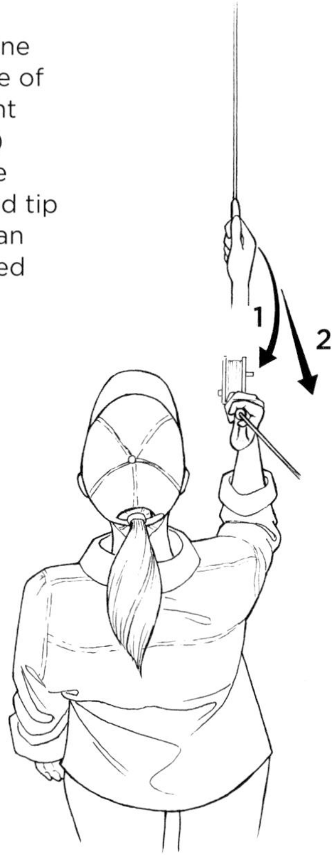

Figure 11-3. When directing your fly line back barely outside of your rod tip, a slight curving tip path (1) returns your fly line back behind the rod tip more efficiently than a straight but angled path (2).

forward cast, your hand and rod tip have completed an oval—when viewed from above (figure 11-4). If you widen the oval as you continue this movement, that oval becomes a circle.

Using curving movements to offset the fly line. In most of the casting discussed thus far, your fly line has been moving in line with—and beyond—your rod. Yet with a curving rod path, you are able to direct the fly line off to one side of the tip to move that line in an even wider circular path than the rod tip is making.

If you take this one step further, you can offset the fly line from the rod to the extent of bringing the line back below the tip. To do so, you start the back cast with the rod tilted slightly to the side and very slowly bring the fly line back below the rod tip on that side—barely above the water. If you use continuous motion to swing the rod tip back up to vertical, you can make a forward cast before the line extends in back. Some people have referred to this as an *air roll cast*. This is a useful option when you have little room behind you. If your fly touches the water to anchor the line momentarily as you rotate the rod around for a forward movement, you are moving into the realm of *spey casting*.

If you bring the line back even lower, so low that it comes back on the water, you are making a basic *roll cast*. If you learned to cast on a pond, you may have learned this cast first—before even learning to make a back cast. Instead of bringing your line back slowly in the air, you bring it back slowly on the water, stop with the line falling just back from the rod, and make an overhead forward cast.

COMBINING TWO CASTING PLANES

Perhaps the most common way to offset the back cast from the forward cast is to change the plane of movement. Sometimes the direction of a prevailing wind, the weight of a saltwater rod, a big hook flying close to your head,

Figure 11-4. Continuous oval rod tip movements pave the way for other curving tip paths.

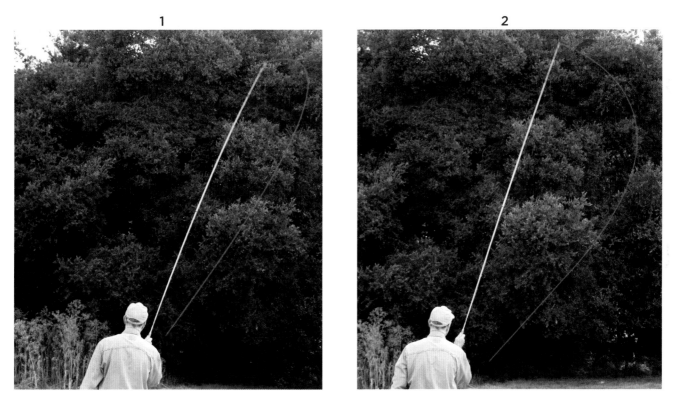

Two back-cast examples offsetting the fly line: (1) A curving tip path helps bring the line back off to the side of the rod, and (2) slow, under-powered movement makes it possible to bring the line back beneath the rod tip.

or weight on your fly or leader give you reason to make a horizontal back cast before coming forward with a more traditional overhead cast. Joan Wulff once referred to this technique as a *constant pressure oval,* whereas Mel Krieger popularized it as a *Belgian cast.* Keeping the fly line moving under constant tension when changing the plane of a cast also utilizes a smooth curving movement of your hand and rod tip.

CHANGING THE DIRECTION OF THE CAST

You combine two casting directions when you pick line up off the water in one direction and lay it back down in another. When casting short, you can do this with a series of false casts by turning your upper body a little farther to the side with each cast until you are facing the direction of your next cast. With more line, you can make your back cast with the rod tilted to the side over one shoulder then circle the rod tip behind you

to cast forward off the other shoulder in a different direction.

However, another technique illustrates even better how to use circular rod movements to change the casting direction. This cast, which is growing in popularity among anglers who use double-handed rods, is sometimes called a *circle cast.*

To illustrate this cast, let's say you have just waded out into a river and turned to your left to face slightly downstream. Your shoreline should be visible on your left. Fifty feet of your line is straight on the water in that direction. Your rod tip is low to the water and pointed at the line.

You start a clockwise "circle" by lifting both the butt and tip of the rod—the tip a little higher—up and out toward the middle of the river. This part of the circle helps you to lift as much line off the water as possible (figure 11-5). Your circular path of hand and rod tip continues down and back under toward the shore again—picking

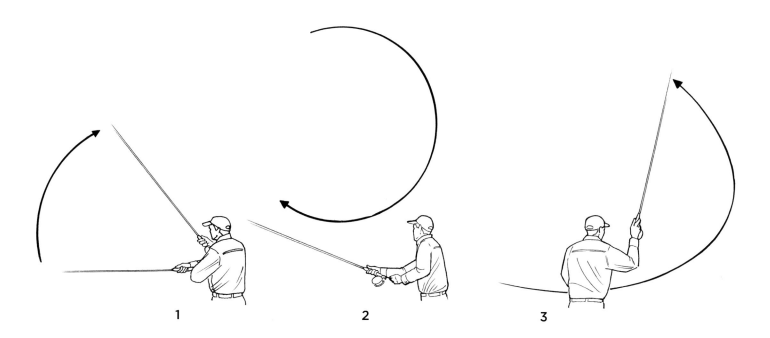

Figure 11-5. In a circle cast, the circle movement starts by (1) lifting the line off the water and finishes by (2) speeding up to throw the line upstream (to the caster's right). Then the rod is (3) swung around and lifted upward in position to make a roll cast across stream.

up speed—to finish pointing back toward the original layout of line. This acceleration as you bring the rod tip down and under lifts the remaining line, leader, and fly off the water to land again slightly upstream from you in what is called an *anchor point.*

As the leader and fly land, you swing your lowered rod tip back across to your right side and lift the tip to one o'clock in preparation for a roll cast across and somewhat downstream.

REVERSING THE ORDER OF CASTING MOVEMENTS

Varying two movements may mean changing the order in which they occur. Sometimes there is an advantage to reversing the order of your casting strokes by starting with your forward-casting motion to deliver the fly behind you, then using your back-casting motion to present the fly to the fish (figure 11-6). For example, you may want to start with a forward cast away from the

fish to visually guide your back cast into a small space between branches behind you, or use that stronger forward casting motion to drive a cast into a wind coming from behind you, or, most often, to keep the fly line moving back and forward on your non-casting side away from the wind direction. Easterner Mark Sedotti impressively features a version of this cast at fishing shows across the country.

These casting movements represent only a few of the most obvious combinations that are available to you. I know several excellent casters who have become so enamored of the possibilities for combinations that they make a study of every specialty cast they have read or heard about. My purpose here, however, has been to select some of the movements and combinations that are most useful to serve as a point of departure for starting your own on-water problem solving. You are limited only by your imagination.

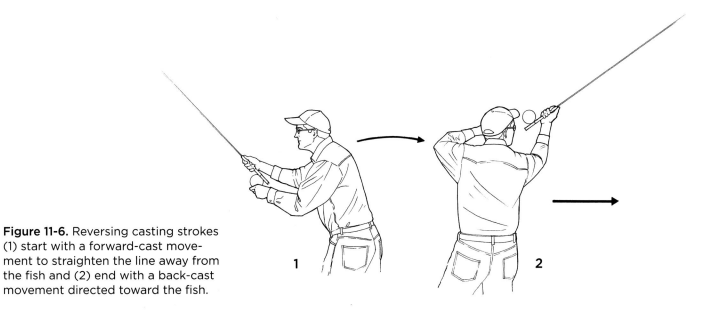

Figure 11-6. Reversing casting strokes (1) start with a forward-cast movement to straighten the line away from the fish and (2) end with a back-cast movement directed toward the fish.

CHAPTER 12

APPLYING ROD MOVEMENTS TO YOUR FISHING

You have been learning how to vary your rod's movements. In doing so, I believe you have also been learning how those movements can change what your fly line does. This knowledge forms the basis of the approach I have been teaching for solving your own casting problems while fishing. All that remains is to start applying this approach to some typical casting problems.

In this chapter, I describe some of the most common casting problems I have experienced in over sixty years of fly fishing. I have separated these problems from my own suggested solutions in the hope that you will take your fly rod outside to work out your own best solution before reading mine. So, you might read the first casting problem, use your fly rod to work out your solution, read my solution, then go on to the second problem. What I consider most important is that you go through the thinking process of trying to use the rod movements you have been practicing to solve problems.

CASTING PROBLEMS I HAVE FREQUENTLY EXPERIENCED

Casting Problem #1. While fishing your way along a wide spring creek, you move from a riffled section to a stretch of smoother water that invites a longer cast. As you extend line to make a fifty-foot cast, you notice that your loop is starting to tail slightly. How do you vary your rod's movements to keep your fly from catching on the leader when making a cast of this distance?

Casting Problem #2. As you continue fishing along that calm water with moderately long casts, your emphasis is on delicacy—dropping your fly gently to the water. At one point, however, you notice that you have softened your presentation so much that your loops have started to widen and open up more than you want. How do you move the rod differently to tighten up your loops again?

Casting Problem #3. As you wade up the middle of a brush-lined mountain stream, you see a good rise well back under an overhanging alder branch to your right. You realize that you need to slide your fly back under that branch and land the line a little upstream of your fly to avoid drag. As a right-handed caster, what rod adjustments do you make to get your fly into that fish?

Casting Problem #4. Fishing up one side of a wide mountain stream you come to a deep pool. The lack of surface activity leads you to rig a yarn strike indicator with leader weight to present small nymphs as far across stream as forty to fifty feet away. What adjustments do you make in your up-and-across stream casts to minimize the tangling of weight, flies, and indicator?

Casting Problem #5. Your bonefish guide is poling you around one end of a mangrove-lined island when the wind starts hitting you from your casting side. At that moment, you and your guide spot a big bonefish approaching from the windy side at one o'clock. There is not enough time for the guide to swing the boat into a better position for casting. You need to make a cast that will move your line on the left side of the boat to prevent hitting your guide with the back cast. Describe the cast you select.

Casting Problem #6. When the tide is right later that day, your guide walks you and your fishing companion out onto a flat that bonefish regularly move across.

Unfortunately the sun angle and direction of bonefish movement force you to cast into a headwind. The wind disturbs the water and disrupts visibility enough that the fish are within fifty feet before you can spot them. What adjustments do you make to present your weighted bonefish fly to these fish?

Casting Problem #7. As you start your morning casting for silver salmon on a coastal Alaskan river, you are experiencing moderately strong winds hitting you on your casting side. The river is a little too deep to wade across. How do you adjust to the prospect of casting all day in those winds with a 9-weight rod?

Casting Problem #8. You are walking down along the bank of a spring creek and notice a good fish rising in quiet water beyond a faster mid-stream current. The water is too deep to approach closely, so you will need to make a forty-foot cast with some line landing on the faster current tongue. Your only approach is to present the fly down-and-across stream. What adjustments do you make in this cast?

Casting Problem #9. As you walk slowly down the right bank of a wide spring creek, you see fish rising forty to fifty feet across stream in currents with subtle variations in speed. You decide to make a cast that is directed across stream and want the end of the fly line, leader, and fly to land a little downstream of the rest of your line. Describe how you make that cast.

Casting Problem #10. As you continue fishing that spring creek down to the next bend, you come upon a few fish rising steadily below you in water with subtle current variation. To avoid drag, you decide you need to cast at an angle that is more downstream than across. You also want to concentrate the slack just beyond your rod tip to be able to feed line into a downstream drift.

What rod adjustments do you make to achieve this presentation?

Casting Problem #11. You are fishing for steelhead on a wide riffle of a western river with a floating line and wet fly. The slippery rocks and fast water keep you close to shore and the willows behind you prevent you from making as long a back cast as you would prefer. The current swings your wet fly down below you on your left. How do you use your rod to change direction and get your longest cast out to a down-and-across angle?

AL'S SOLUTIONS TO THE ABOVE CASTING PROBLEMS

I hope you have taken my suggestion to use your fly rod to come up with your own solution before reading mine. With some of these problems you will need to wait for a windy day. Undoubtedly, there will be some differences between our solutions. You may even want pick up your fly rod again and compare the solution I offer with your own. You may still prefer yours. The important thing is that you are using the problem-solving process you will need to use when on the water—identifying the problem, observing what happens to the fly line as you adjust, modifying that adjustment, and observing again.

Solution #1. Many fly fishers control casting loops well on thirty-foot casts but find that their loops start to tail on longer casts. When I see this happening in my own cast, I first make sure I am starting my forward cast smoothly without any "give" or looseness in my wrist. If the loop still has a tendency to tail, my primary adjustment is to change the loop shape by widening the angle of my cast. I do this specifically by adding a little backward drift to my back-cast stop. This also adds a little stroke length, which can help by providing a little longer path for my rod's tip. If I know beforehand that I will be fishing on a wide spring creek, I eliminate any loops or knots in the

butt section of my leader and make sure my line-leader knot is small and smoothly tapered without any rough spot on which the fly can catch.

Solution #2. Occasionally my loops open up too much on long trout casts. This most often happens because my concern for delicacy overrides my concern for tight, fast loops. As a result I get a little relaxed with my casting stroke and the loops start to open up. The adjustment that works best for me is to stop my forward and back casts more abruptly and use a short haul timed with my thumb press on the rod. I may also narrow the rod's angle of rotation a bit.

Solution #3. This is a common small stream casting problem. Underpowering a curve cast with a sidearm delivery would give you the curve you want but moves the line too slowly for use under branches. What I would do is to tilt my off-side cast down to horizontal and stop the forward cast hard enough so the rod tip sends the fly farther around to land downstream of the line—an off-side positive curve cast.

Solution #4. Here you need to avoid tangling the leader weight, hooks, and indicator material. Tangling can occur from making a hard stop at the end of a casting movement or just from moving the back cast and forward cast through the same space. So whenever I make long casts with weight on the leader, I most often adapt by making a sidearm back cast and move smoothly up into an overhead forward cast. When using leader weight, I try to make this cast with continuous movement and wide casting loops.

Solution #5. In this situation you need to move the fly line back and forward on the left side of the boat from seven to one o'clock (the front of the boat is twelve o'clock). I have tried every version of an off-side or back-

hand cast I could think of for this common bonefish casting problem, including canting the rod just slightly and even casting with my non-dominant hand. Most of these casts don't provide enough strength for some of the winds you encounter on the flats. The cast that works best for me is to reverse my casting strokes, making a forward casting motion for the back cast and a back-cast arm motion to drive the fly forward to the fish approaching at one o'clock. Somehow it took me longer than it should have to realize that I could make that cast without looking back. (You need to keep your eyes on the fish.) Although a back-casting movement out to the fish doesn't seem strong, the low hand position allows me to use strength from the shoulder to add to a well-timed haul. The toughest part for me to learn was stopping the rod butt sooner than I thought I should. So, when a Bahamian guide says, "Use your back cast, Al," this is what I do.

Another important element when casting from a boat is making sure your thumb and forefinger circle the fly line that is shooting out through your rod. This enables you to stop the line flow and start stripping without any loss of control. This is critical when being poled, because drifting toward the fish creates slack in your line. Delaying or mishandling the first strip will cost you fish.

Solution #6. Usually your guides try to avoid having you cast into a headwind. The obvious adjustment is to tilt the forward cast downward and stop hard with a haul to drive the forward cast low into the wind. Yet I found when doing this that the splash of the bonefish fly spooked approaching fish. If I slowed the cast or raised the target line much, the wind would catch and collapse the cast. However, I found that there was a precise angle (slightly downward) and speed that combined to drive the cast into the wind and turn the fly over without spooking the fish. With the fish so close, I kept my one or two false casts off to the side a little to extend the line before changing direction to drop the fly. Facing this casting problem reminded me how important it is to be able to vary the up/down tilt of your cast.

Solution #7. When experiencing a strong, constant wind from the casting side, I have learned to look for a place to cross to the other side. When that is not possible, as in the situation described, I have learned to alternate between two casts: (1) reversing the casting strokes; and (2) switching the rod to my non-dominant hand to do the casting. I have taught myself to cast well enough with my non-dominant hand to reach seventy feet with a double haul. Alternating the arm I cast with in these two casts and using as effortless a motion as possible with both casts allow me to cast all day in such a wind without developing extreme soreness in either arm. Of course, fighting big salmon adds to that strain. Whenever the wind backs off for a few moments, it is a treat to make a few conventional casts.

Solution #8. This is another common problem you might experience on either a mountain stream or spring creek. You need to land your fly line on a tongue of moving water while achieving as long a drag-free drift as possible in the quiet water beyond. My favorite adjustment for this type of spot is to make a high-angled forward cast by tilting the cast back (i.e., pile cast). As soon as I have stopped my cast, I drop the rod tip to the water. The high-angled forward cast both buys a little time to do some things with the rod and guarantees that the line will land with slack. Lowering the rod tip to the water helps pull the fly line downward into a more vertical drop and lowers the near part of the fly line to the water.

As soon as I have dropped the rod tip and line to the water, I make a big upstream mend of the line that has landed. The fly and leader have not landed yet, so in one sense this "water mend" is part of the presentation. At any rate, this mend sets up a drift with the fly line on the faster water but as far upstream from the fly as possible. In such water I often rig my dry fly with an extra long tippet—four to five feet—to take more time to drop the fly to the water and uncoil before being dragged downstream.

Solution #9. Here you are fishing across some current variation with a fairly long cast and want the far part of the fly line angled or curved to land downstream from the rest of the line. The cast I prefer for this situation has four elements—a tight casting loop, a downstream reach during the cast, a quick aerial mend back upstream, and a quick drop of the rod tip to the water. The tight loop gets the fly line out quickly and efficiently. Angling your hand and rod tip downstream during this cast starts the line angling slightly downstream. A quick aerial mend back upstream shocks the fly line so as to sharpen the angle in the far part of the line and leader back upstream from the fly. Dropping the rod tip to the water prevents the fly line from bouncing back toward you in the air. I prefer the angled layout of line this cast gives me to the slack I get from bouncing the line back by overpowering the stop.

Solution #10. This is a cast I often use to fish a dry fly downstream ahead of myself when a spring creek has tricky, subtle currents. Aiming the cast more downstream than across, I stop the forward cast in the air and pull the rod back toward myself (an aerial mend in a different direction) before dropping the rod tip to the water. When done properly, the fly line and leader should land fairly straight except for a few waves of slack just beyond my rod tip. This gives me slack where I need it for feeding line into a drift that moves the fly down to a rising fish.

Solution #11. In this situation, I wish I were using a double-handed rod. Yet an increasing number of fly fishers are learning to use spey casts with single-handed rods—and that is what I would do here. I would use the circle cast, first raising the rod to lift line off the water, continuing the clockwise circle up and around, then accelerating down and back under toward shore to lift the fly off the water and land it farther upstream. Then I would bring the rod back across to my right and lift it to one o'clock to make a roll cast across and downstream.

How did you do on those problem situations? Or perhaps I should ask, How did I do? At any rate, these are just a few of the many casting problems you might experience—problems that can be solved by varying your fly rod's movements in ways you have been practicing. I'm sure you can think of other casting problems.

The circular movement in this circle cast (1) starts after raising the rod tip to begin a slow, clockwise movement which (2) speeds up through the lower half to reposition the fly line to the right in preparation for a roll cast across stream.

CHAPTER 13

THE CONTINUING JOURNEY TO A BETTER CAST

Our journey together—this search for a better cast—is drawing to a close. I suspect we have covered some ground that was familiar to you and some you had not been over before. I hope you have become excited about working on your cast in new ways.

Perceiving the cast differently. I believe you may now be looking at an overhead cast differently than you did before. You may now think more about the importance of moving the rod tip and fly line along a straight path, and marvel that people can move so differently to achieve that path. You may even see your fly rod as the adjustable tool that makes it possible to achieve straight-line flow with different casting styles, rod tapers, casting distances, and fishing presentations.

Moving the rod differently. Much of what you have done here is learn how to move the rod differently to adjust to such differences. First, you identified and worked with several types of rod movements, varying each as you changed from short to long overhead casts. You learned how the techniques of drift and the double haul contribute to changing these rod movements. In the pivotal chapter of the book, you learned how to vary one movement at a time and watch the effect on your fly line. Then you varied two movements together and began to understand how various specialty casts came into being. Throughout this process, I believe you began to see how these rod movements can help you to solve casting problems when fishing.

Solving the problems differently. I have often seen fly anglers with nice casts who were completely dependent on their fishing guides or someone else for ways to adjust their casts to present the fly differently. My hope is that you will now be less dependent than before on other people for such help. I hope that you can observe a casting problem in your fishing and know how to zero-in on a solution—that you now have a practical approach for solving it by systematically varying what you do with your rod.

You did some problem solving here by using these rod adjustments to work through a few written fishing problems. The next application is to do the same thing when fishing. This problem solving should tie in naturally with the problem solving you already do after the cast as you experiment with unique combinations of line feeds, water mends, and retrieves.

So, although the overhead cast and certain specialty casts may not have been new to you, learning to systematically vary the movements of your fly rod and the layout of your fly line may well have been. That is what I consider to be most unique about what has been offered here.

Continuing the journey. As long as you apply this problem-solving approach to casting problems in your fishing, you are continuing the journey we have started together. Perhaps you have already started to develop a love for creating your own combinations for more effective casts than you learned here. As you do this, you are moving beyond the scope of this book. Perhaps you will also continue this journey in another way—by delving further into circular tip paths, changing direction, and anchoring line in the study of spey casting.

I have tried to introduce you to fly casting as I see it—various styles, various rod adjustments, and even various tip paths. Hopefully, when you see a caster using different movements, you won't immediately say, "That's wrong." What you will say instead is, "That's different. Why is it working so well?" Not long ago, I enrolled in one of Al Buhr's excellent spey casting classes. The student next to me in that class was Joan Wulff. I guess the really good ones never stop being a student, and a better cast is a lifelong pursuit.

ACKNOWLEDGMENTS

Many people have contributed to this book in one way or another. A few need to be mentioned specifically.

First I wish to thank Tom Rosenbauer of Orvis for encouraging me to submit my fly casting perspective to The Lyons Press for publication. I also need to thank Chuck Easterling, Gordon Judd, Don Simonson, Dusty Sprague, and John Till—master casting instructors from various regions of the United States—for reading through a draft of this manuscript and enriching it in various ways with their own perspectives.

I particularly appreciate the contributions of two people who are special to me—Julie Ecklund and Rex Agbulos. The artistry of Julie's drawings and Rex's photographs have given life and meaning to my words.

Finally I thank my wife, Barbara, for the love and support that makes such prolonged effort possible.

INDEX

ABOUT THE AUTHOR

Al Kyte started fly fishing in 1945 and was teaching fly fishing classes and writing about the sport by the 1970s. He is the author of *Fly Fishing—Simple to Sophisticated,* and has written various articles on fly fishing and fly casting.

In the early 1990s, Al was among the first group of instructors selected from across the country to organize and oversee the national fly casting instructor's certification program for the Federation of Fly Fishers. As a long-time faculty member at the University of California, Al brought to fly casting the perspective of a teacher, coach, and researcher. He was selected to Northern California's Fly Fishing Hall of Fame and to the Orvis fly fishing advisor team. Al lives with his wife, Barbara, in Moraga, California.